Seeing the Charade:

What We Need to Do and Undo to Make Friendships Happen

Carol Tashie, Susan Shapiro - Barnard
and Zach Rossetti

conclusion by Jamie Burke
original art by Kristína Holúbková

Inclusive Solutions: Nottingham UK
2006

Seeing the Charade:

What We Need to Do and Undo to Make Friendships Happen

© Carol Tashie, Susan Shapiro-Barnard and Zach Rossetti
ISBN 0-9546351-3-2

Published by Inclusive Solutions UK Limited, July 2006

Original Art © Kristína Holúbková
Conclusion © Jamie Burke

This book is filled with stories from the authors' personal and professional experiences. Except when both a first and last name is given, the names have been changed to respect the privacy of the students, teachers and families whose stories we are using.

To honor the free and open exchange of ideas, permission is given for photocopying of any and all pages of this book. We ask only for acknowledgment of the book's title, authors and publisher on all copies.

To arrange a workshop on friendship, please contact the authors at cztashie@yahoo.com

Printed in Nottingham, England
by Parker and Collinson Limited
Church Street, Lenton, Nottingham NG7 3FH
www.parkerandcollinson.co.uk

Contents

WELCOME

Charade
1.   An absurdly false or pointless act or situation

Seeing the Charade
1.   To learn, think, and act in new ways
2.   A willingness to challenge the status quo

Thanks so much for picking up *Seeing the Charade: What We Need to Do and Undo to Make Friendships Happen.* This book is truly a labor of love, written after close to 20 years of learning, teaching, and questioning this thing we call friendship.

Carol, Susan and Zach met while working for the University of New Hampshire. Although we had different roles, we all worked with schools and families to support children with disabilities to become fully included students, valued for who they are and the gifts they bring to their communities. One by one, we came to realize that friendship (or the lack thereof) was the elephant in the room. Everyone knew it was a problem, but nobody wanted to talk about it. And so we, and others, started to talk about it. And more importantly, we started to listen and watch and learn.

Because our jobs allowed us to spend so much time in schools, we were able to observe in classrooms and talk to students. And so we sat in classrooms, notebooks waiting to be filled with our ideas for supporting friendships for the students we were observing. But instead we found ourselves filling the pages with the reasons why friendship was such an elusive goal. How the educational supports that were put into place to help students were actually hurting them socially. How much of what was being done in the name of "friendship facilitation" was really just a charade.

To check out our assumptions, we started talking to students. And parents. And teachers. And colleagues. And, yes, friends. They all helped us solidify our beliefs and our knowledge. This book explores those observations, conversations, and beliefs.

Each one of us comes to our passion for friendship from a slightly different place. Carol is a peace and justice activist with a professional career in education. Susan is a homeschooling mother, former classroom teacher, and adjunct faculty member. Zach is a doctoral candidate and older brother to Todd, who experiences disabilities. Together and separately we do workshops and teach courses on inclusive education and friendship. We decided to write this book as a way of sharing what we teach and what we love.

How We Learned What We Learned

We are not the type of people to sit and ponder a problem. We are much more doers than philosophers. And so we realized that the answers to our questions were not to be found inside our own heads, but in the very schools in which we were spending our time. And among the very students we were observing.

And so, as we began trying to understand what was happening in classrooms, we did three things, all connected and possible for anyone interested to do themselves.

First we spent time observing what was actually going on. On invitation from teachers and principals, we sat in classes with one question in mind: "Why does this student have no friends?" We sat in the "catbird seat," a chair in the back of the room where it was possible to simply watch and listen to what was happening in the class. It was eye opening and gave us great insight.

Secondly, we would leave the catbird seat to wander around the classroom and talk to students. We did this with students kindergarten through high school seniors, and we asked them open-ended questions about their classes, the curriculum, and adult roles. The answers to these questions (which we will share throughout the book), confirmed what we had been seeing and led us to formulate many of our ideas and beliefs.

Lastly, we brought together groups of students and asked them for their thoughts, insights, and suggestions. Boy, did we get an earful. You will read some of their wisdom throughout this book.

So that's how we gathered most of what we learned. We also spoke with teachers and parents and great thinkers in the school and community inclusion movements. But mostly we watched, talked to, and listened to kids.

About The Language We Use

Although this book is written by the three of us, we decided to use the first person, singular and plural, wherever possible. You will see there are places in the book where the word "we" is used to describe the work we have done collectively. There will also be places where the word "I" is used, but we do not identify which one of us is speaking. This is not to be mysterious, but instead to make the flow of reading easier.

You will also see that the book is filled with stories. Except when *both* a first and last name is given, we have changed the names to respect the privacy of the students, teachers, and families whose stories we are using.

Although we use aliases, we did not change the stories. Each example is one that comes from our personal and professional experiences. And from each example comes a wealth of insight and understanding.

We hope this book will be read by parents, teachers, paraprofessionals, students, related service providers, principals, recreation directors, coaches, camp counselors, you name it! But to keep the flow and language consistent, we uniformly use the term "student" to talk about anyone of public school age. We seldom identify the disability label of the student we are writing about, unless it is pertinent to the storyline. Our experience has given us the opportunity to spend time with and know students with a wide variety of labels, and so chances are *yes, we are talking about your student!*

About the Organization of the Book

This book is a written record of the teaching we do on friendship and inclusive education. If you have attended any of our trainings, you will most likely recognize a story or two (or three or four). And like our workshops, this book is organized in a very specific way.

We write first about why so many students do not have the social lives they want and deserve. We call this section *Barriers* and it frames the issue of friendship from the perspective of what stands in the way of students becoming friends. We strongly encourage you to read this section with an open mind and a critical eye to what is happening for the students you know and love. It is not the easiest information to digest, for it challenges many of the practices that occur in schools today. But please do not skip this section. We believe it is the heart and soul of the work we are doing.

Upon learning about the barriers, many people ask how they can avoid or overcome them in their schools. Wonderful question! And while this book cannot give you all of that information, we do offer you resources to learn more about best practices in education and community supports. For information about some of our favorite books and movies, check out the resource list at the end of the book.

The next section is called *Strategies*. Please do not be tempted to jump right to that section. The strategies we offer are not earth-shattering, for the most part they have been known and used by the field for years. While we believe we have offered some new ways to frame them, we still discourage you from only reading and working on the strategies. Implementing the strategies, without spending time thinking about and overcoming the barriers, will not give you the results you want and your students deserve.

People We Want to Thank

Oh my. When we sat down to think about the people we wanted to thank for helping us learn about friendship, we were overwhelmed. Do we mention Lucas, one of the first students who taught us about giftedness? What about the young people who were kind enough to meet regularly with us, sharing our pizza and their wisdom? Or the parents who encouraged us (in no uncertain terms) to put friendship at the top of our priority list? We cannot list everyone, and yet we don't want to leave anyone out.

And so we thank *all* of the students who have taught us the true meaning of belonging. *All* of the families who showed us that love can change the world. *All* of the teachers who opened their classrooms and their hearts. *All* of the school administrators who created caring communities for each and every student. *All* of the school personnel who did the hard work and allowed us to learn from them. *All* of our colleagues who challenged us to think and rethink our ideas and assumptions.

By name we want to thank Jeff Strully, Marlyn and Jocelyn Curtin, Michael Sgambati, Norman Kunc, Emma Van der Klift, Cathy Apfel, Candee and Katie Basford, and the late Herb Lovett for teaching and inspiring us every step of the way.

We thank Jamie Burke for giving the book its last words. No book could end on a truer or more hopeful note.

We thank Kristína Holúbková for her amazing art work, created during classes at Charles University in Prague. Kristína's artistic insight into our human family never ceases to amaze us.

We thank Ellen Frisina for the gift of editing and proofreading. All remaining errors are our own.

We thank Derek Wilson and Colin Newton at Inclusive Solutions for publishing this book and allowing us to say what we believe without censorship.

And most importantly, we thank our families and friends, for without them our souls and lives would be empty.

Peace and Hope
Carol, Susan and Zach

INTRODUCTION TO BARRIERS

First the good news. The world is starting to catch on to what so many people have been saying for decades - friendship matters for everyone. Mastering math or knowing how to cook a meal is all well and good, but without people to share your life, they are hollow treasures indeed. Friendship is what makes the world go 'round and everyone needs and deserves full and rich social lives.

Families and professionals are starting to talk about friendship being an essential part of students' lives. No longer do we hear (okay we still hear it, but not quite so often) that "schools don't do friendship." Instead people are beginning to see that belonging not only makes students' lives more fun, it also paves the way for greater learning. It is a rare school team that does not give at least some time and thought to the issue of supporting a student to have greater opportunities to meet people and develop real relationships. That is good news.

Now for the bad news. Many of the friendship strategies used to support students' social lives are based on manuals that prescribe how to "do" friendship or programs that offer to take care of it for us. And in many ways, it is understandable that such programs are sprouting up. Once we identify a problem (Liana has no friends), it is only the hard-hearted among us who would not try to come up with a solution.

And thus we look at strategies and programs that promise, if not friendship, then friendly and friend-like opportunities. Promise fun. Promise a chance to be around, or even paired with, other students. Promise to solve the problem of "no friends."

But wait. It isn't working. Loneliness is still the most common complaint for large numbers of students, and despite programs and manuals, many students still do not have real friends. And so we must ask: Have we identified the problem or just one symptom of the real problem?

Liana has no friends. But why not? What is standing in the way of others seeing her gifts and beauty? How is it that she does not have the social life she desires?

(Now just in case you are worried, this is not the time in the book for a discussion of all of the things *about Liana* that make it harder for her to make friends. In fact, nowhere in this book, or in anything else we have written, will there be any discussion of this topic. Sure, there are things all of us could do to make ourselves more interesting, appealing, likable to potential friends. But despite our many "faults," we all still have friends. So this is not about "fixing" Liana to make her more desirable. Liana, like you and me and everyone else in this world, is fine just the way she is.)

Friendship. What's the Real Problem?

So what is the real problem? If we believe that the problem is the fact that Liana has no friends, then there is some logic in looking into strategies and programs that sell the promise of friendship. When the problem is no gas in your car, you look for places that sell gas. Isn't this the same thing?

Perhaps, but what if the real problem is a crack in your gas tank? Then having no gas would be only a symptom of the problem and filling up with gas no real solution at all. In fact, by buying gas (over and over and over again), you may actually never find the time or have the money to identify the real problem. And you might begin to believe that this old car of yours is really destined to get only five miles to the gallon.

Similarly, what if by enrolling Liana in a friendship program we stopped trying to find out the true reasons she has no friends – and began to believe that she is destined to never have any real friends after all?

We believe that Liana's lack of friends is just a symptom of the real problem. And in order to identify the real problem we need to ask *why* she has no friends. What is standing in the way of real friendship? What are the barriers to friendship for Liana?

We believe Liana has no friends because of the way people view and therefore treat her. We believe that the cards are stacked against Liana, by the very systems and structures designed to "help" her.

Consider this. Liana is a middle school student. She is enrolled in 7th grade general education and attends classes with a paraprofessional who accompanies her throughout the day. She also receives a variety of support from related service providers and the school's inclusion facilitator.

To work on her goal of counting and understanding money, Liana starts off her day in the school cafeteria, working with her paraprofessional and "peer helper" to count the change from the vending machines. Each day the "helper" rotates so that no student has to miss first period more than once a month. (No student other than Liana that is...)

After working in the cafeteria, Liana goes back into class, sometimes at the end of first period, sometimes not until the beginning of second. Since the class schedule also rotates, the class she enters could be any one of her subjects. Whatever the class, Liana begins her literacy lessons, reading words from a worksheet or from flashcards placed on common objects around the room. It is often difficult for Liana to concentrate on this work as, depending on the subject, the other students could be working in groups or listening to a lecture. The paraprofessional often has to redirect Liana's attention to her own work, and sometimes must take Liana out of the classroom so that she can fully attend to her task at hand.

Because Liana gets support services from a variety of related service professionals, she is pulled from class several times each week. Again, due to the rotating schedule of 7th grade classes and the constancy of the related service professionals' schedules, the times she leaves classes are independent of the class agenda. Often Liana does not want to leave, especially when she and her classmates are involved in a cooperative activity or an exciting lesson (or just goofing around).

When she stays in class, Liana works on a parallel or modified curriculum, depending on the subject. Supporting Liana to learn the information that everyone else is learning is a low priority for her team, so Liana uses these lessons to enhance her functional and "Activities of Daily Living" skills. During a class discussion, it is common for the teacher to bypass Liana or ask her a "functional question" (What day of the week is it?) rather than one based on content. During tests, Liana leaves the room so she does not distract the other students. During lunch, the paraprofessional sits with Liana, reminding her to "use good manners" and sometimes keeps Liana inside during recess so that she can wash her face and hands before returning to class.

Had enough?

Liana is just one of the thousands of students who, though considered "included," are really more *out* than *in,* and perhaps more importantly, viewed by classmates more as visitors than actual members of the class community. How do we know this? We talked to some of Liana's classmates and asked them questions such as, "Who is that?" referring to the paraprofessional; "Where is she going?" referring to Liana leaving class; "What does she do?" referring to Liana's class work. And from their answers we got an overall impression of benevolence ("We all love her"), charity ("I work with her"), and marginalization ("She isn't really like us").

So why does Liana have no friends? She is simply not seen as part of the *pool of potential friends.*

What is this Pool of Potential Friends?

In most social situations, we size up the people around us to see who we want to talk to, sit next to, get to know better. Imagine yourself entering a room full of strangers. You may look around and decide (perhaps subconsciously) who you would like to meet. You may decide based on clothing (everyone is dressed in business suits except you and a "potential friend" who are both in jeans). You may decide upon hearing bits of conversation (one person is talking about hybrid cars and you are interested in that). You may decide based on who seems to be well-liked by others in the room or by who is sitting alone. Whatever your way of deciding, you scope out the room and begin the process of figuring out who is in your pool of potential friends.

Now imagine Liana's classroom. Sure Liana is in the classroom — sometimes. But her likelihood of being seen as part of the pool of potential friends diminishes every time she leaves the classroom, comes in late, works outside the curriculum, or is managed by an adult other than the teacher. And so when friends are chosen, Liana is out of the running.

Now some people explain the fact that Liana is left out of the pool by saying how "cruel kids can be" or by talking about the inevitability of cliques. But we think that it is not the students that need to change. It is the systems we have put and kept in place in the name of (special) education that are not working.

Why does Liana have no friends? Because we have created a system, that even when *called* inclusion, really serves to separate and isolate Liana from her classmates.

Is it is hopeless? Is Liana destined to be outside of the pool forever? No! But we have to take a good hard look at the reason why Liana has no friends - the real problem - and then work real hard to solve it.

Solving the Problem

Solving this problem, while not simple, is doable. It involves taking an honest look at the ways in which the student is being educated. It means not settling for inclusion in name only. It means helping adults understand the ways they can help or hinder the student's membership and belonging.

Solving the problem means getting the right people involved. Asking classmates for ideas on how the student can be more included in all aspects of the class and school. Helping students recognize common ground, while appreciating differences. Talking openly and honestly and teaching students to advocate for themselves and each other. Not asking students to "be Liana's friend" but asking them to help you figure out why and how real friendship can happen.

And most importantly, it means putting intentional time and energy into identifying the *real* problem, and not getting sidetracked by promises of an easy-fix.

Solving a problem is never easy. But it is near impossible if we do not acknowledge what the true problem is.

So join us as we explore, one by one, the barriers we believe are the real reasons why friendship is not happening for so many students, and offer some alternatives to help all students wade, dive, or jump into the pool of potential friends.

BARRIERS:
WHAT TO UNDO

But He's Not Really in Our Class

I was once in a 5th grade classroom observing Aaron, a young boy who, among other things, was identified as having no friends. Sitting in the catbird seat, I watched as an amazing teacher engaged students in a variety of fun and meaningful lessons. Earlier in the day, the teacher had confided in me how frustrated she was that Aaron had to leave the classroom to receive special services. She felt this was not good for Aaron or the class community. But since she had no choice, she had worked the schedule to make sure he left during the least interactive times of the day. Today it was "daily oral language" and as the students began working quietly at their desks, Aaron left the classroom with the occupational therapist.

Minutes later the silence of the classroom was disrupted by a student who loudly exclaimed that his uncle had just returned from Venezuela! Noting the excitement this generated, the teacher took advantage of this unexpected learning opportunity and challenged the students to spell Venezuela and find it on the map. Eventually she had the students break into small groups and write letters to the uncle asking questions about the language, culture, geography of this country. What a brilliant teacher! While the students begrudgingly did "daily oral language," they were thrilled to be using proper grammar, punctuation, and spelling (the goals of daily oral language) to write these letters! The room was buzzing with energy and, I must admit, I was caught up in the excitement when Aaron walked back into the room.

He left as the students were silently doing "daily oral language." He returned to a roomful of enthusiastic chatter about Venezuela.

Venezuela?

The teacher quickly recognized Aaron's confusion and did everything she could to relieve it. She explained about the student's uncle. She had him join a particularly active group and asked that they include him in the work they were doing. She checked in with him from time to time. She did everything possible, but the damage was already done.

Aaron already felt like an outsider. Lost. Confused. Sad. Angry. Embarrassed.

The group he joined already felt inconvenienced by having to stop what they were doing to bring Aaron up to speed. They were annoyed. Frustrated. Resentful. They wondered why Aaron always had to be in their group.

The class community had already been damaged by the exclusion of one of its members. If Aaron's membership was tenuous, who would be next?

Not the kind ideal conditions for friendship.

In or Out?

It probably goes without saying that students need to be together in order to develop respect, mutual interests, and real friendships. However, for many students with disabilities, even those whose placements are considered general education classrooms, their school days still consist of separate places and lessons. These students continue to be "pulled out" of their classrooms to receive services from therapists and special educators, and these pull-outs negatively impact their ability to make friends. Any student who leaves the classroom misses important opportunities to connect with classmates around content, shared experiences, and activities. He returns to the classroom unsure as to what he missed. And, as described in Roberta Schnorr's classic article, "Peter...He comes and goes..." (1990), other students view him as someone significantly different from themselves.

Find Out for Yourself

Pulling students from classes serves as a barrier to developing social relationships. But you don't have to take our word for it, you can find out for yourself.

First spend some time in the catbird seat. Observe what happens when a student is taken out of the classroom by a therapist or teacher. How does the student respond? Is she upset? Resigned? Resistant to leave? Or perhaps the opposite. Don't be fooled when a student seems happy to leave the classroom. It is often an indicator that she does not feel successful or welcome or a sense of belonging among classmates. And our response should be concern not satisfaction.

Now pay attention to how the rest of the class responds? This is a pretty good indicator of how a student's classmates see her in relation to others. Do they shout out "Where are you going?" or do they seemingly ignore her removal? Do they stick up for her if she resists or do they either disregard it or "play teacher" and tell her she has to leave. Do they ask to join her or shy away when she is told she can bring a friend?

(Wanting to join is extremely common when students are in kindergarten through 2nd or even 3rd grades. But as students grow older, their interest in joining decreases. Older students are more sensitive to social dynamics while younger children tend to enjoy the adult attention.)

Okay enough observing, it's now time to ask the experts. While your answers might differ, here are some of the most common answers we get when asking students about a classmate who is being pulled out of class:

Question. "Where is Lucas going?" Answer. "He is going to *his* classroom." Q. "But what is this room?" A. "This is *our* classroom."

Q. "Where is Lucas going?" A. "He is getting special help."
Q. "What do you do when you need help?" A. "I get it from our teacher in the classroom."

Q. "Where is Lucas going?" A. "The sped room." Q. "What's that?" A. "That's the classroom for retarded kids." Q. "Do you ever go there?" A. "No way, it's not for kids like me."

Q. "Where is Lucas going?" A. "He was bad."

Q. "Where is Lucas going?" A. "To play."

Q. "Where is Lucas going?" A. "I dunno…."

Students have spoken loud and clear. They tell us that while Lucas spends time in their classroom, he is not really a part of the class. He is "he" and they are "we." And of course this negatively impacts friendship. From the answers given above, is it any surprise that Lucas is not really in the pool of potential friends?

Alternatives to Pull-Outs

So what can we do? We can avoid this barrier by rejecting the notion that some students must leave the classroom in order to learn. We can work together to ensure that all of a student's necessary supports are delivered within the context of the general education curriculum and classroom. We can advocate for related services to be integrated into the class curriculum or provided before or after school.

Teachers have the power to develop classroom environments that allow each student to participate in and learn from all lessons. For example, when teaching a science unit on photosynthesis, the teacher can provide students different ways to develop and demonstrate their knowledge. After conducting experiments, some students can write lab reports while others can develop photo essays. A group of students can create a mural representing the role of plants in the health of the planet. Other students can develop a game show in which students write questions and answers, serve as the host, or participate as contestants. Teaching with an emphasis on different avenues for involvement recognizes that all students can learn and that we value the different ways in which they do.

Parents have the power to withstand the pressure to "fix" their children and must recognize that having a child leave the classroom for "special this" and "special that" negates many of the positive affects of a student's membership in the classroom. The practice of pull-outs contributes to a student's isolation and serves as a significant barrier to the development of true and meaningful friendships.

Dangerous Assumptions

Assumptions. We all make them, despite the fact that a warning about the dangers of assumptions is embedded into the very word itself. (Remember giggling when you first heard that "If you 'assume' you make an 'ass' out of 'u' and 'me'."). And yet we continue to disregard this caution and keep right on making assumptions every day.

While it would be great to say, "STOP making assumptions," that's probably not realistic. So instead, what if we agree to work hard at making the *least dangerous assumptions*?

Assumptions are most dangerous when they limit or prevent people from achieving their greatest potential. And for many students with disabilities those kind of dangerous assumptions are very much a fact of life. See if you can find the dangerous assumption in the following situations:

Mo's team decides she should not attend any high school science classes as her IQ score indicates that she would not understand the material being taught. Instead she spends those periods cleaning tables in the cafeteria so that she can someday get a job in food service.

During a spirited discussion on slavery, the teacher asks students to voice their opinions on its modern day implications. When Trey raises his hand, the teacher asks him to tell the class his favorite food. His classmates are silent during his answer and then quickly resume their boisterous discussion when he is done.

What do these scenarios have in common? What are the dangerous assumptions that are made and how do they potentially limit students' access to curriculum, learning, career choices, and friends?

Mo's IQ score says nothing about her interests or her capacity to learn science. Trey's inability to speak does not mean he does understand or have something important to communicate about slavery. When we make those assumptions we suffocate learning opportunities and disrespect students.

In 1984, Anne Donnellan introduced the concept of the least dangerous assumption as it related to people with disabilities. In 1995, Donnellan and Martha Leary proposed the "Criterion of Least Dangerous Assumption" which states that in the absence of absolute evidence, it is essential to make the assumption that, if proven to be false, would do the least amount of harm. It continues by explaining that the "absence of evidence can never be absolute evidence of absence."

Consider it this way. If you were to go fishing and not catch any fish, there would be two assumptions that could be made. First, you could say "There are no fish in the lake since I did not catch any." Or you could say "I did not catch any fish but that doesn't necessarily mean there are no fish in the lake, it just means I did not catch any." The first assumes that since you did not get any concrete evidence of "fish in the lake" there must not be any. The second assumes that your lack of concrete evidence (fish) doesn't prove anything about what's actually in the lake.

The same holds true for students with disabilities. Imagine a student who does not have a way to communicate her thoughts or tell us how much she is learning. Because there is an absence of concrete evidence, her team has to make decisions based upon assumptions. And they have two choices. They can assume that "what you see is what you get" and that this student does not know anything, is not understanding anything, and will not learn much in the future. Based on this assumption, they may decide to educate her in a way that reflects those assumptions (perhaps segregated classes or regular classes with low or no expectations).

Or they could make a different assumption. They could acknowledge that although they do not know how much this student understands, there is no reason to assume she is not understanding everything. With this assumption, they would make decisions about her schooling that would reflect those high expectations and she would be a valued member of all general education classes. And of course, they would never stop working to provide her with a variety of strategies and supports to communicate her thoughts and knowledge in ways more easily understood by those around her.

One scenario, two different assumptions. Which one is the least dangerous? Which one would be most devastating if proven wrong?

Assumptions and the Pool of Potential Friends

As it becomes more obvious how dangerous assumptions can impact a student's ability to reach her greatest potential, let's examine how dangerous assumptions also serve as barriers to being seen as part of the pool of potential friends.

To do this, imagine a 6th grade classroom. While sitting in the catbird seat we observe the teacher directing the class to begin journal writing. The students reach into their desks and take out their black and white composition books and begin writing. The paraprofessional working with Jared brings him a large box filled with brightly colored magnetic letters. The box is decorated with Sesame Street characters and the words "for ages 3-5" are easily visible across the front.

In order to the get the scoop from the experts, we leave the catbird seat and wander around the room quietly asking students what Jared is doing. Their answers come as no surprise: "We are working, Jared is playing." "He never does what we do." "My little sister plays with those same toys."

What do these answers tell us? Listen to the language the students use. *We* are working, *he* is playing. *He* doesn't do work like *we* do. It doesn't take long for the barrier to become crystal clear: There is an *us* and there is a *him.* Because of the assumptions made about Jared's inability to learn and participate in the class curriculum, Jared is seen as an outsider by his classmates. He is not really a member of the class. And by definition, if you are "not one of us" then how can you be seen as part of the pool of potential friends?

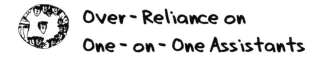 ## Over-Reliance on One-on-One Assistants

Michael Sgambati, a young man whose schooling included the near-constant presence of a one-on-one paraprofessional, presents at conferences about the ups and downs of his school career. He never fails to get the audience howling with his story of being a student and having his "aide" walk him to the men's room. "I was in there just a short while when she started knocking on the door," Michael says with dramatic flair. "I ignored her at first but she kept knocking and saying, 'Michael are you okay? Michael are you still in there?'" As the audience starts chuckling, Michael delivers the punch line: "I finally got so frustrated I just yelled through the door, 'Leave me alone, I don't need a wife.'"

While that story never fails to get a big laugh from the audience, "It wasn't very funny when it happened," recalls Michael. "She was a very nice woman, but I was a kid and I didn't want any adult to follow me around all day long." Michael then goes on to share the realities of having a paraprofessional: classmates' taunting or indifference, teachers' lackadaisical attitudes toward his learning, and the ongoing struggle to reconcile his strong need for independence with the constant presence of an adult. "One of the best parts about graduating from high school was knowing I would not have an aide anymore."

Michael is not alone in his experiences of having an adult assigned to him throughout his school day. The assignment of a paraprofessional is one of the most common supports provided to students who are educated in general education classes. And yet this practice is jam-packed with problems, both educational and social.

The One - On - One Paraprofessional as a Barrier to Friendship

While there are educational reasons to question the use of one-on-one paraprofessionals (we especially love, and recommend you read, the work of Michael Giangreco and Mary Beth Doyle), we were interested in learning if this role also serves as a barrier to friendship. So we went to our most trusted sources of information – students – and learned how the near-constant presence of an adult can dampen, and even drown out, any possibilities for real friendships to take hold.

Take 6th grader Ani for example. Her team told us that other students did not want to eat lunch with Ani because of her personal eating habits and her challenging behaviors. They asked us for suggestions on how to change Ani's behavior so that she would be better accepted by her peers. So what did we do? We sat down with a small group of students and asked them to tell us what was going on at lunch. And boy did we get an earful! Rather than complain about Ani's behaviors, they were adamant that no one wanted to eat lunch with Ani because no one wanted to sit with the adult who was always by her side. It was not that they didn't like this paraprofessional, in fact, some students expressed a real fondness for her. But they were pre-teens, and they didn't want an adult — any adult — sitting with them at lunch. And when we asked what should change, they rolled their eyes (as only adolescents can do) and exclaimed, "Tell Mrs. Atkins to eat with the teachers and leave Ani alone!"

Is this a unique situation? We do not think so. In fact, we have been asking students these kind of questions for years and usually get very similar answers. Here are some of the most common answers to the question "who's that" when pointing to the paraprofessional:

That's Jonathan's helper. She's Nadina's teacher. She does Alex's work for him. She makes Leslie behave. She gives Marietta things to keep her busy. That's Roberta's aide. That's his mother. His grandmother (heard from a 1st grader). Her bodyguard. Her friend. I don't know who she is.

What answers would you get if you asked students the same question?

A word of caution. Getting honest answers from students requires an honest approach to asking the questions. If students believe you will be defensive or are asking only to justify the status quo, they will be less likely to tell you the truth. If students believe you truly want to know what they think, they will be more open with you.

The Paraprofessional as a Friendship Support

I walked into a 3rd grade classroom as the students were free-writing and noticed one student, Anita, who was writing a story called "My Two Crazy Teachers." Intrigued, I stopped and asked her to tell me about her story. With a huge grin, she told me she was writing about Ms. Lenore and Ms. Liakos and how great it was to have two teachers who were fun and interesting and slightly "off the wall."

Ms. Lenore was the 3rd grade teacher. Ms. Liakos was the paraprofessional, who was assigned as the one-on-one assistant to a student named Mattie. But for Anita, all she cared about was having two wonderful teachers working in the classroom with her and every other student!

We cannot end this section without saying a few words about the ways a paraprofessional can be incredible educational and social supports for all students in a classroom. While we stand by our cautions and concerns, we also know that when done well, a paraprofessional in the classroom can pave the way for all students to flourish academically and to grow in their appreciation for each other and their class community. A paraprofessional can make all of the wonderful learning opportunities in school accessible for all students, bringing the vision of educational excellence and equity a bit closer to reality.

There are numerous resources to help you learn more about the positive role of the paraprofessional (again, we recommend anything by Mike Giangreco or Mary Beth Doyle) and so we offer you just a few words of wisdom to begin you on this path.

Even if a paraprofessional is specifically assigned to one student, make sure the role is defined as a teacher's assistant rather than a personal aide. Our rule of thumb is this: The role of the paraprofessional is to support the classroom teacher to be the best teacher he/she can be for all students in the classroom.

One of the best thing we can teach all students is how and when to ask for help. If a paraprofessional is by a student's side all of the time, the opportunities to learn this are severely diminished. Instead, the paraprofessional can roam around the room helping all students so that each student can learn to identify the need for help, request it of the most appropriate person (classmate, teacher, paraprofessional), and wait his turn.

A paraprofessional is often in a perfect position to pay attention to the natural sparks and opportunities for connections between students. A paraprofessional can notice which students have a budding affinity for one another and connect students who share common interests or experiences. By observing and acting upon these opportunities for connections, paraprofessionals can play important roles in supporting relationships.

It is easy to believe that the way in which your team has developed the role of the paraprofessional serves only as a support and is not a barrier at all. Many teams will tell us that students in the classroom see the paraprofessional as "just another teacher" who is truly is there for all students. If this is so, congratulations. Good for you and good for your students. But just to be certain, why don't you ask the students what they think. Just to be sure.

 ## Well, It Looks Like Friendship...

It is essential that we don't waste any precious time or energy misleading ourselves about a student's social status in the classroom. And it is easy to be misled. If you walk into a classroom and see two students sitting together and involved in a joint endeavor, you might conclude these students are friends. After all, they are sharing time and space and clearly engaged in shared activity. What could be better? And if you probe no further, you may leave confident that the goal of friendship is met and check that off the student's long list of educational priorities.

But wait. What if we are wrong? What if what we are seeing is not friendship but peer support? Or a teacher-directed buddy system? Or social skills training? Then, by maintaining the pretense that this is friendship, we actually create a new barrier – the charade that everything is just fine. And if everything is just fine, well we don't have to put anymore of our time and energy into it, do we?

We call this barrier *Well, It Looks Like Friendship* and it can take many forms.

As noted, seeing these two students together may actually be the practice of peer support, one student helping another in some way. Is there anything wrong with this? No! Peer support (or peer teaching) is a time-honored and valuable strategy to help students learn and grow from one another. But peer support, while a great way for students to work together, is not friendship. Friendship occurs when students discover common interests and develop a mutually satisfying relationship. Peer support is the kind of help one student gives to another, sometimes directed by an adult. And while it is true that friends often provide support, and peer support can sometimes develop into friendship, they still remain very different kinds of relationships.

So how do you know if it is friendship or peer support? Simple — just ask the students. The question, "So what are you two doing?" will yield a wealth of insight. Answers such as, "I am helping her", "I am teaching her", "The teacher asked me to work with her", will guide you to believe you are witnessing peer support.

One more point about peer support. One of the many things we have learned from Norman Kunc and Emma Van der Klift, is how important it is to make sure that all students have the opportunity to *give* as well as *receive* support to/from their peers. While the act of peer support is hierarchical ("I am helping you") and has the danger of perpetuating stratification in the classroom ("I am the helper, you are the helpee"), this danger is eased in classrooms that ensure that every student regularly serves both roles. And what a wonderful challenge to pose: how to notice and support all students' gifts and talents!

What about other ways in which we can be misled? As noted, the two students working together could be engaged in a social skills training activity. And while we are not opposed to teaching students social skills, we also know that one's social skills have very little to do with one's social life. (If this does not ring true, please visit a middle school cafeteria!) And so, engaging students in social skills training may appear to be friendship or friendship-in-the-making, but it is not real friendship.

Another practice that may fool us is the adult-directed buddy system. Many teams, in sincere attempts to mitigate a student's lack of friends, will institute a buddy system for a particular student. These often take shape as "recess pals" or "lunch buddies," where a student is linked with one or more classmates, often on a rotating basis, to have someone to eat with or play with at recess. You may even see charts with these titles hanging on classroom walls (Yikes!). While the intent of these systems is admirable, they serve as a barrier in at least two ways.

First, they are part of the overall way in which we can be fooled into believing the student has friends. If you see the student eating lunch with other students, or going out to recess with a classmate close at hand, it is easy to assume friendship. Secondly, they serve as a serious barrier to the student being part of the pool of potential friends. If an adult needs to legislate who will sit or play with you, it is much less likely you will be seen as a desirable friend in your own right.

The final form this pretense can take is one that deserves its own section. It is perhaps the biggest charade of all – *Friendship Programs.*

The Charade of Friendship Programs

Ten years ago "Friendship Programs" were few and far between. Today, they seem to be cropping up in schools and communities all over North America. An informal survey of families who have enrolled their children in such programs reveals a common thread: "I know friendship programs are far from ideal, but sometimes I feel like they are the best I can hope for."

Are friendship programs really the best we can hope for? Must we enroll the students we care about in special buddy programs in order to give them the opportunity to be around others their own age, even if those others are given class credit or salary or "brownie points" for their participation? Are we obliged to settle for "less than ideal" as the only antidote to loneliness? And if we don't, are we sacrificing children at the altar of educational philosophy?

Let's examine friendship programs as a barrier from two different perspectives. Then let's see if it is possible to turn the concept into a viable strategy.

We have already made the point that anything that gives the appearance of friendship without really being friendship is a problem. Friendship programs illustrate this reality and then some. Consider that the very nature of friendship programs require time and energy and often money to run. Given the fact that time, energy and money are available in limited quantities, friendship programs not only lull us into complacency, they also sap resources that could be used to develop more individualized supports for genuine friendships. Interestingly, friendship programs, especially those with prominent titles and supporters, do a tremendous amount of fundraising in our communities. From walk-a-thons to celebrity-studded charity events, these programs bring in large sums of money to create, maintain, and promote their programs. So, in addition to these programs serving as a barrier to real friendship for children, they perpetuate the notion to our entire community that people with disabilities are not in the pool of our potential friends — they require specialized programs for their social and community participation.

Paying for a Friend?

Friendship, by definition, does not involve payment of any sort between friends. As our parents told us when we were young, if you must pay someone to like you, to spend time with you, then that person is not a real friend.

So, what does this have to do with friendship programs? The students who are asked to be the "special friends" or "buddies" in such programs are, more often than not, given one kind of payment or another. And while that payment is seldom money, it is often school credit, community service hours, citizenship awards, or great college recommendations. Whatever form it takes, it is still payment. And friends do not get paid for being friends.

Such disingenuous relationships are damaging for all involved. The student who has a paid buddy is, in essence, being told that he is undesirable and unworthy of a true (unpaid) friend. Why else would you need to pay someone to spend time with him? And what about the student who is paid for her participation in the program? She is being taught a lifelong lesson that some people are not friendship-material — not part of the pool of potential friends — and she will most likely carry this prejudice with her for a long, long time.

One interesting note. Ask someone who runs a friendship program if the students know that their "buddies" are paid for their participation. Chances are the answer will be negative. Ask them why not. Chances are you will hear that it would "hurt their feelings" if they knew this fact. Need we say more?

So, is there any way to turn a friendship program into a positive strategy for supporting students to develop genuine relationships? Perhaps. One way would be to hire students not as "peer-buddies" (or paid companions) but instead as relationship facilitators. Students could in fact continue to be paid for their involvement in the program as their role would no longer be "buddy" but instead as a bridge builder or support provider to help that student become more involved with people and activities of his choosing. This would require training in the art of supporting friendships, but it would be time and money well spent.

Disability Seen As Deficiency

Remember when we were kids and our parents told us not to stare at the person who used a wheelchair, a cane, or a hearing aid. Aren't we glad those days are over with? Or are they? Not long ago I was in the airport waiting to catch a plane home. When the pre-board announcement was made ("…any passenger needing extra time can now board…"), a woman using a wheelchair wheeled through the crowd and onto the jet-way. A young boy, no more than 5 or 6 years old, innocently asked his mother, "Mom, why do wheelchair people get to go on the plane first?"

Isn't that a wonderful question? What an opportunity to teach a young child about people first language ("Well, honey, *people who use wheelchairs*…") and to enhance his budding curiosity about the world we all share ("People get around in so many different ways, don't they?"). What an opportunity to help create the kind of world we all want to live in, right?

But what did I hear coming out of his mother's mouth? (Hold on to your hats, and remember this is 2006 and not 1956!) In response to this wonderful question, this mother, in a harsh whisper, said, "Stop staring! And just be thankful that you have two healthy legs."

And so it goes. Once again, a child's natural wonder with the differences we all share is turned into a reinforcement of society's belief that disability is not simply a difference, something that makes the world a richer and more interesting place to live, but it is a deficiency, a problem to avoid, prevent, and, if possible, fix.

Not sure you believe this is so? A friend of ours just told us that the incidence of children born with Down syndrome in California is way below the national average. Why? It seems that prenatal testing has given parents an early peek at their child-to-be and when they see "Down syndrome" they choose to opt out. Because the world would be a much better place without people like that…????

Thanks to Norman Kunc we call this barrier *Disability Defined As Deficiency.* And when we believe that a disability is a deficiency, then the ways in which we educate, interact, and respond to students with disabilities will reflect this belief. The student is no longer Trey, the youngest Johnson brother, the boy who loves building castles with Legos, can't get enough black raspberry ice cream, and wants to be an astronaut. Instead he is the low functioning autistic. Or the Downs boy. Or the behavior problem. He is seen in terms of his label, and many of his qualities are transformed into deficits. And through our actions, we pass these beliefs on to others in Trey's life. Classmates included.

Not many of us would intentionally teach children that people with disabilities are deficient. But children learn this nonetheless. And sadly, they learn it from us.

Disability defined as deficiency is the belief that leads to many, if not all, of the barriers to friendship. It leads us to make dangerous assumptions about competence and ability, which leads us to make damaging decisions regarding curriculum, class participation, and adult support.

Perhaps not as dramatic as the desire for a world free of people with Down syndrome, but damaging just the same.

 ## Culture of Tolerance

Consider these two 5th grade classes, both of which are reading Ron Jones' book *The Acorn People* about a camp for children with disabilities. One teacher, after having the class read the book, gives students the assignment to write about their good fortune of having healthy bodies and how they would feel if they were one of the campers in the book. The second teacher, before beginning the book, asks the students to check the date of publication (1976), and do some research on society's view of people with disabilities in the mid-seventies. He then engages the class in a discussion of the comparisons between that time period and today, especially as it relates to where children with disabilities lived, played, and went to school. As the class reads the book, the teacher makes frequent references to this research. As an assignment, the teacher gives the students a choice to either write an essay about these differences or to rewrite sections of the book using today's knowledge and the values.

It is not uncommon to hear of schools and classes that work hard to instill in their students the value of "tolerance of differences." And while the intent is almost always admirable, it is our belief that the promotion of "tolerance" actually places another barrier in the path of genuine and reciprocal relationships. It is not enough to simply "tolerate" the differences among us, for tolerance implies a hierarchy of value. One prizes good health, but tolerates a cold. So what, then, is implied when we strive for schools and classrooms that tolerate disability?

Let's take a closer look at the two teachers above. Both have students with disabilities in their classes, both chose the book as a means to encourage a discussion about diversity, both expressed hope that this lesson would help the student with disabilities feel more included in the class community. But when both teachers were asked how they felt about the student with disabilities in their classes, some significant differences emerge. The first teacher responded with sadness, expressing that she felt sorry for the child and his family and hoped that other children would treat this boy with kindness and sympathy. She said she structured her class in ways to ensure that this student had helpers with him throughout the day, and each day she assigned a student to play with him at recess. She believed that having this boy in her class would help the other students learn to appreciate how much they had (how lucky they were) and hopefully be more compassionate to those who were "less fortunate."

The second teacher expressed very different sentiments. While admitting that he worried about being a successful teacher to the student with disabilities, he expressed his excitement to be teaching in a time when children with disabilities could be included in general education classes. He was constantly amazed at how much this student was capable of and said he was learning to be careful about placing preconceived limitations on any child. He hoped that all of his students were learning to appreciate the ways in which we are all the same and hoped they would generalize that thinking to all people in the world.

The barrier of the *Culture of Tolerance* can be easily overcome. Teachers and administrators can create schools and classrooms that express in both word and deed that disability is an integral part of our human community, it is neither better nor worse, it just is. These schools and classes would respect and value the differences in all of us, and demonstrate it through curriculums rich in multiculturalism, lessons taught through multiple intelligences, and cooperation valued over competition. They would reject the notion of traditional "disability awareness" activities, which tend to teach students to view disability as something either undesirable, heroic, or as greater than all of the person's other characteristics. In these environments, the seeds for friendships between all students would be sown.

In order to create classrooms that truly value diversity, teachers can embed the history and contributions of people with disabilities into their standard lessons. When studying inventors, teachers can highlight Temple Grandin, a woman with autism who is an inventor of livestock management techniques. Novels about and memoirs of people with disabilities can be studied (for example, *Stuck in Neutral* (2000), *My Louisiana Sky* (1998), and *I Raise My Eyes to Say Yes* (1989). When teaching about civil rights, teachers can include Ed Roberts' contributions to the independent living movement, and the 1988 student protest at Gallaudet University. When discussing important artists, teachers can show the work of Christy Brown (or the movie *My Left Foot*, 1989) and Dan Keplinger (or the documentary *King Gimp*, 1999). Students can learn how many of the most influential people in history had disabilities, including President Franklin Roosevelt, Albert Einstein, and Stephen Hawking, and that many important inventions, such as the telephone, were invented to support people with disabilities.

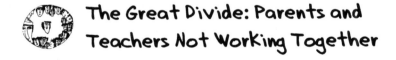

The Great Divide: Parents and Teachers Not Working Together

When Marlyn Curtin, a well known and respected advocate for friendship and community supports, first began thinking about facilitating friendships for her daughter Jocelyn, she asked Jocelyn's teacher to send home a list of the names and phone numbers of students in the class who Jocelyn liked and who liked her. This request was met with resistance. "I'm sorry Ms. Curtin," she was told "We can't do what you ask. It would violate our school's rules about confidentiality if we gave you students' names and phone numbers."

Unfortunately, it is not uncommon for families and schools to feel at odds with one another when they begin thinking about friendship. Sometimes it is the family who feels that the school should put friendship into the child's IEP and make it happen in school. Sometimes it is the teacher who wonders why the parent is not doing more at home. Sometimes it is a disconnect between the school and family, both believing in the importance of friendship, but neither wanting to broach the subject for fear of opening a can of worms. Sometimes it is an outright difference of opinion as to whose job it is to take make things happen, or if friendship is truly possible at all. Whatever the reason, too often families and schools report dissatisfaction in how they work together on this very important issue. And subsequently, little or nothing gets accomplished.

But it doesn't have to be that way. Let's go back to the example above. When Marlyn requested a list of students names and phone numbers, she was thinking only of making connections with Jocelyn's potential friends. She did not intend to challenge the school's rules or regulations. But Marlyn's request raised the red flag of confidentiality, the school couldn't honor her request without compromising their mandate of student privacy. And while they respected her, they just couldn't comply.

It was a stalemate, one that could potentially damage relationships between the school and the family.

We all know how easy it is for differences to turn into standoffs. The more I stake my position, the more you fortify yours. Arguments seldom bring two parties closer together, they generally serve to push people further (metaphorically) against opposite walls.

And yet in their groundbreaking book *Getting to Yes: The Secret to Successful Negotiation* (1983), Roger Fisher, William Ury, and Bruce Patton illustrate how disagreements can, in fact, lead to solutions - if they are no longer framed as "me against you" but instead "us against the problem."

In order for "us against the problem" to work, two questions are critical. What is the real problem and what are our non-negotiables? (Non-negotiables are those things that you are not able or willing to ever compromise or bend on.)

Let's go back to Marlyn's example. Both the family and school had their positions. Marlyn's position was that she wanted the school to give her names and phone numbers. The school's position was that they could not breach the privacy of their students. These positions were in opposition to each other. Marlyn vs. the school. Framed like that, a resolution would only come if one of them backed down from their original position.

But they framed it another way: us against the problem.

First they figured out the problem. In this case the problem was that Jocelyn was not able to come home and tell her mother which classmates she liked and wanted to invite over to her house. And without a way around this problem, Jocelyn's educational and social life would suffer.

Then they discussed their non-negotiables. Marlyn's was clearly that she wanted a way to contact Jocelyn's potential friends. She was not going to compromise on this, as she believed that it was essential for Jocelyn's happiness and well-being. The school's non-negotiable was their pledge of student privacy and confidentially. They had this written into their professional code of ethics and would not compromise no matter how compelling Marlyn's arguments were.

You can see how this could easily lead to a stand-off. But they had agreed on the problem and therefore were committed to using their collective energy to come up with a solution to the problem, without compromising their non-negotiables. And they did.

Their solution: Marlyn would send to school an empty address book for classmates to write in their names and addresses if they were interested in getting together with Jocelyn after school. And the end result was the same as originally requested – communication between Marlyn and Jocelyn's classmates was facilitated – but no school rule had to be broken.

Problem solved.

Can this strategy work in every case? We don't know. But what we do know is that when families and schools are not able to work together, this serves as a huge barrier to students getting the supports they need to have the educational and social lives they deserve.

Role Modeling the Us - Them Divide

When I was young, my parents repeatedly told me to "do as I say, not as I do." And whether they were talking about smoking or cheating or treating someone with respect, I didn't buy it then, and I don't buy it now. I know actions speak louder than words and that young people, in particular, pay much closer attention to what we do than to what we say. Which is why as teachers or parents or just responsible adults, we must be mindful of our power to serve as role models for our beliefs and values.

There are so many examples of the ways students learn from our deeds. Consider this most extreme case in point.

I was observing a middle school student in homeroom. Students were seated in rows and the teacher was reading aloud the day's announcements. Jordan, the student I was observing, was the only student not seated, he was walking back and forth between the rows and at one point he brushed up against some of the other students. "Oh gross, he touched me," one student called out. "Sick, disgusting, get away from me," cried another.

But the teacher kept on reading "….bring soup can labels to school tomorrow…."

I was struck less by the students' comments than by the teacher's silence. This silence served to condone the students' remarks and sent the class a message of, if not approval, at least complicity. And I had to wonder, would she have remained silent if the students had responded this way to being touched by a student who was African American? Or Muslim? Or gay?

As Martin Luther King said "In the end, we will remember not the words of our enemies, but the silence of our friends."

Students learn from their teachers all the time, even when we don't think they are paying attention. Every decision we make has consequences. What we teach, how we teach it, what books we choose, what stories we tell (and don't tell), what examples we use (and ignore), who we choose in class, how we interact with students with disabilities. All of this is noticed by our students. They notice and learn. And what they learn is not necessarily what we *say* we want them to learn.

We might *say* we are trying to instill a sense of motivation by showcasing a high achieving student's work on a regular basis. But ask other students what this is teaching them and they might use words like favoritism, shame, and resignation. And that rather than being encouraged, they are learning that certain students are more valuable (and valued) than others, that the status quo will not and should not change, and that discrimination is a way of life.

Role Modeling and Friendship

Now let's turn this critical lens to role modeling as a barrier to friendship. If we believe that students learn from our actions, then we must also believe that how a student is treated by his teachers influence (positively or negatively) the ways he is perceived by his classmates. And those perceptions, in turn, influence his status in the pool of potential friends.

Consider the following examples we have seen in schools. As you read them, please ask yourself: What is the teacher trying to convey? What might the students be learning instead? How does this influence the way they see the student as a possible friends? For we believe, in all of these examples, the adults' intentions were pure. If we asked them to explain what they were trying to convey, we believe their sentiments would be positive and caring. But in all of these examples, the adults' intentions and the lessons learned by students are very different.

◎ Teacher speaking to paraprofessional: "He looks sad today. What kind of day is he having?"

◎ The class is discussing the history of the eight-hour work day and the teacher asks a student with disabilities, "Do you like ice cream? I like ice cream."

◎ Paraprofessional talking to the teacher: "This is too hard for her, she's not going to be able to handle it. I'm going to take her to the cafeteria early."

◎ A spelling quiz is handed out to every student in the class except for Hector, who has a label of autism.

Let's examine these examples a little more closely.

When a teacher talks about a student in front of his classmates *("He looks sad today")*, it communicates several messages that can serve as barriers to friendship. Classmates may begin to believe the student doesn't understand (or even hear) what is being said to him, and therefore they may begin to talk about, rather than to, him themselves. Classmates may assume that the student doesn't mind being talked about, that this is the way he wants to be treated. They may begin to think that the student is not able to communicate, even ignoring signs to the contrary. And perhaps most dangerous, they may come to believe that this student is not worthy of the kind of respect they would bestow on others.

When adults talk to a student in a manner or voice not appropriate to her age *("Do you like ice cream?")*, classmates can get the impression that this student is not really a member of the group and, in fact, has more in common with much younger children. When adults ask questions that are independent of the classroom context or existing discussion (ice cream vs. history), classmates learn that the important conversations they are having are not appropriate or of interest to that one student.

As noted earlier, students can also learn from a teacher's silence. When the paraprofessional calls the shots (*"This is too hard for her, she's not going to be able to handle it"*) classmates get the message that the paraprofessional is really the student's teacher and the student is not a real member of the class. When the student is taken out of the classroom (*I'm going to take her to the cafeteria early"*), this reality is once again reinforced, leading to a damaged sense of community and belonging.

It is not only through words that these dangerous messages are conveyed. When Hector does not get the spelling quiz, classmates get a clear message about his status in the classroom. While at first some students might balk and remind the teacher to give a paper to Hector, they may soon learn to ignore both the slight and Hector.

These are just a few examples of how students learn from how we behave in real situations. These examples are not meant place blame, but instead to instill in all of us the importance of being mindful of how our actions speak much louder than our words.

We encourage you to notice how similar examples in the lives of the students you know and love serve as barriers to students seeing each other as capable, competent, and valued friends. And to pay attention to what you are teaching with your every word and deed.

 ## It's Not My Job

Consider this: The neighborhood park needs to be cleaned up. Everyone knows it needs to be cleaned. It has needed cleaning for years. But no one is taking the lead. No one is organizing a cleaning crew. No one is gathering the tools. And so I lament, *"The park needs to be cleaned up. Why is the park not cleaned?"*

Could it be because no one is taking ownership? Does everyone, including me, believe it's not my job??

No surprise that the park never gets cleaned.

We don't really need to say too much about the barrier of *It's Not My Job*. It's as obvious as the dirty park. Because as great as it is to recognize that there is a need (to clean the park or support friendships), it really does take someone to step up and begin the work. And that person has to be you.

Now, we know the realities. We have worked in schools for many years. And we are parents and family members ourselves. We *know* that time is precious and priorities are many. We know that you want to help make friendships happen, but isn't there someone else who should, could, be doing it?

First, we address teachers. The political powers that be are working hard to convince us that the only way to improve our schools is through testing and accountability. And so while your priority may be creating a just and caring class community where all students can and will learn, you know that your students are not being tested on how well they work together. And you know that friendship and belonging are not part of the fill-in-the-blank assessments. And so you wonder if supporting friendships is still your job.

When you started teaching, you rejected the old adage of "you don't have to like me, you just have to learn from me." And because you know that unless children feel a part of the learning community they will not achieve to the best of their abilities, you have strived to make your classroom a place where children's needs are met and achievement can soar.

So you know supporting friendships for students is your job. Creating the conditions for relationships to bloom is your job. Maintaining a community where all feel welcome and supported is your job. Paying attention to those students who need a little extra help to belong is your job. Giving support to those students who need more than a little help to develop friendships is your job.

You know your job is more than teaching reading or biology or math or advanced physics. Your job is to teach children how to be productive and healthy and caring citizens of our world. And you can't do that if you don't recognize the essential role that social connections play in a students life. For belonging leads to self-esteem which gives way to achievement, learning, and finding success.

Supporting social relationships for students is not something to do once the "real work" of teaching is done. It is the first step in doing the real work. Students cannot learn when their basic needs for belonging are not met.

Supporting friendships for all students is part of all teachers' jobs.

Now, parents. Hopefully you just read what we wrote for teachers and are enthusiastically nodding your head. But you must know we are not stopping with teachers. It is your job as well. You see, we think something has happened to disrupt the natural ways parents see their children who have disabilities. We think that educational testing and labeling, and even IEPs, give families the message that everything about their children requires professional intervention. And we worry – oh, we worry very much - that families are getting the message that supporting friendship is the job of trained professionals. People with letters after their names (Mary Smith, F.R.I.E.N.D.) and diplomas on the wall. And that leads many families to answer the "Whose job is it?" question with an answer of "It's the school's job."

We believe it is a family's job to support their son or daughter, brother or sister, to have friends. No one – we repeat – no one loves your child the way you do. No one has the longevity that you have. No one will ever have the relationship that you have with your child. Family bonds are unique and powerful. It's hard to imagine anything stronger.

And so when it comes to supporting friendship for your child, it is your job. No if, ands, or buts. It is your job. Because you love your child and know that without relationships in his life, he will not grow to be the person he can and wants to be. So you cannot abdicate your responsibility, even to the most caring and competent of professionals. Because you love your child.

But can you do it alone? Some have tried, and actually some have succeeded. But we do not recommend it. Supporting friendship takes many hands and heads and, yes, hearts. And so families are essential, but it is wisest to work together with teachers to make it so. Imagine the power of this. Families who love their children working with teachers whose jobs are to create communities. Together they can do just about anything.

So what is the answer? We go back to the un-cleaned park. The answer is someone has to say "it is my job" to make sure the park gets cleaned but to admit "I can't do it alone." Will that someone be you?

It Was Easier in Elementary School

We recently met a paraprofessional who, in the mornings, works in a 1st grade class and in the afternoons moves to the middle school to support Heather in 6th grade. As she tells the story, in the mornings she is "cool." The students all love her and clamor to be by her side. Modestly, she believes that her presence as a one-on-one assistant to the 1st grader actually increases his status in the classroom. But the story is quite different in the afternoon. In the middle school she is anything but "cool." The 6th graders all but ignore her, and they ignore Heather as well. She feels that her presence is not an advantage to Heather, but instead a liability.

We don't need to tell you what we learned from this story. You know that as children grow so does their need for independence from adults. If you have children of your own, you know the sting of realizing that the child who once clung to your side is now too embarrassed to have you drop her off in front of the school. You know that children need to develop this independence and they will do just about anything to achieve it.

So it should come as no surprise that a one-on-one paraprofessional becomes a greater barrier to friendship as children age. Students' natural desires for independence run counter to the educational system's insistence on adult support. And classmates will no longer tolerate the presence of an adult in their midst.

But there is more that changes over time. During our workshops, we often ask parents of young children to tell us how things are going in the friendship arena for their children. We usually see smiles and hear stories of play dates, party invitations, and friends. But then we ask the parents of older students. Instead of smiles they shake their heads, instead of good stories, they share their laundry lists of concerns. Asked to think back to when their children were young, most can remember when friendship was not such an elusive goal. But today? Well, things are not so good.

Why is there such a difference? Why is friendship more difficult as students get older?

The prevailing wisdom used to go like this: As students with and without disabilities get older, their interests and cognitive skills diverge. Their abilities become more dissimilar. The developmental differences become more apparent. And friendships suffer as a result.

But we are here to subvert this convention and offer a new perspective. We believe it is not that students' interests and abilities become more dissimilar as they grow older, but instead, it is their experiences and opportunities that acutely diverge.

Throughout their education, students are continually exposed to all of the barriers discussed in this chapter. They have been taught that students with disabilities are not capable of learning within the classroom. That they need the ever-constant presence of adults. That teachers have little or low expectations of them. That there is truly an "us" and a "them." That disability is not simply another difference, but a deficiency of ability and worth. That friendship programs and buddy lists are necessary. That people with disabilities deserve our pity. That tolerance is the best we can do.

So, why is friendship harder as students get older? Because despite our words to the contrary, every day we teach students to believe that the pool of potential friends is off limits to so many students. Of course this is not our intention, but nonetheless they learn that certain classmates would not make good friends.

 ## Inaccessibility of Transportation and Public Spaces

Ah, sweet sixteen. An important rite of passage for so many young people. Licenses, driving, freedom. Remember when a plan to go see a movie with friends meant two and a half hours of driving around, hanging out? It all felt so important, so cool. But, what happens to the students who can't get licenses and don't cruise around with their classmates?

One of the reasons that elementary school friendships fade in high school is so obvious it's amazing we didn't notice it right away. Most cars cannot accommodate wheelchairs (or other equipment students may have). So if the debate team is going to the local coffee shop to tighten up their arguments, then Sharee can't go along unless her mom or dad drives her, because none of Sharee's classmates has a wheelchair accessible car.

So how do we overcome this barrier? You might say, "Let the classmates borrow the family's accessible van so they can all hang out together." Great idea, but only if the family is comfortable with a teenager driving their (often large, usually expensive) vehicle. Many families do not have the confidence or financial resources to say yes to such an idea.

So what is the solution? We advocate for *all* school buses to be accessible. For states to invest as much in public transportation (fully accessible of course) as they do in streets and highways. For communities to be planned so that cars are less necessary and desired. And we suggest schools recognize transportation as the barrier it is, and support families and students to come up with creative transportation strategies to ensure their full and valued participation in all community opportunities.

Inaccessibility

And even if Sharee can get to where her friends are going, will she be able to get inside?

Consider this scenario. Kelly (who gets around in a wheelchair) and his brothers went to the local movie theater, where they immediately went to their favorite seats. Since there was no accessible seating in the theater, Kelly sat in the aisle. An usher informed the boys that "the wheelchair" was a fire hazard and they had to move to the back of the theater. During the discussion the usher ignored Kelly, talking only to the brothers, and referred to Kelly as "the wheelchair." The usher explained that the reason they do not have accessible seating is because people with disabilities never come to the theater.

Hmmm.....

Situations like this one show how often the onus is placed on the person with disabilities rather than on lack of access or equality in our communities. Is it Kelly's problem that he can't sit where he wants to in the theater or should the theater ensure accessibility for all people?

Intellectually we know the fault lies in society's barriers, and not with the person. But, like the usher, the inverse is frequently communicated or implied. To Kelly, his family, and to his potential friends. And let's be honest, it's hard to be friends with someone who *literally* can't go with you to your favorite places.

The Stigma of the Little Bus

Transportation is not just a barrier that prevents students from getting where they want to go, it also carries with it the stigma of how they get there. Too many schools still use those little yellow buses and the stigma of those buses transfers to the students who ride them. It is not uncommon to hear students call those buses the "tard bus," the "cheese box," or the "sped bus" and none of those are meant as terms of endearments.

And understandably so. Those buses bypass all of the students waiting on the corner and pick up "special" students at their front doors. Convenient on a cold winter's morning, but segregated nonetheless. And where do the little yellow buses go when they reach to school? Often to side entrances, where the students are met by adults and immediately whisked into the school building. Missing out on chances to hang out with classmates before the first bell rings.

A parent we know once enrolled her son (who does not have disabilities) in a summer day camp at their local school. The school provided transportation and on the first day a little yellow bus pulled into their driveway. "Oh my," thought the parent, who quickly ran out to wave the bus on. She was petrified that her son might have seen the bus, for she knew how devastating it would be for him to think this bus was for him.

 **Prejudice**

Consider the difference between these two life experiences:

"When I was growing up the only person with disabilities I ever saw was my next door neighbor's oldest son. He lived in an institution and when he occasionally came home for a visit, my sister and I were warned by our parents to "be careful" around him. We never really knew what this meant — what exactly were we to be cautious of — but we got the message loud and clear. He was "weird" and "foreign" and, of course, "dangerous." I can't speak for my sister, but I carried this message with me for many years. When I entered the world of education and began to meet students with disabilities, I had to challenge the prejudice I was taught at home, in school, in society. And to this day, I know I carry the remnants of that prejudice with me. It is inside of me — in my core — and I need to acknowledge it is there. I cannot change my past, I probably cannot completely eliminate the bigotry that is inside me, but I can control what I do with it. And I know I will have to fight against it every day of my life."

"I grew up as the oldest of six kids, one of whom has disability labels. I grew up seeing the barriers and prejudice my brother faced every day, from moving to a new town so he could be included to having waiters ask *me* what my brother wanted to order. When I went into the field of education I did not need to learn about inclusion, I grew up knowing inclusion. I grew up playing hockey with all of the kids on the block, my brother playing goalie sitting in his wheelchair right smack in the middle of the net. I grew up learning to drive the wheelchair-accessible van so we could all go to soccer games and dance recitals together. I grew up standing up for my brother against teachers who babied him and other students who believed this was fair. I know I am privileged for growing up in my family. I also know that most people have not had the opportunities I had. And so while I sometimes (okay, often) get frustrated and angry when I see the bigotry against people with disabilities, I know that these people have not had the kind of privileged upbringing that I had. They were taught prejudice and now they need to unlearn it. I can only hope that when more and more people have the privilege that I had, the narrow-mindedness will cease to exist."

We end the section on *Barriers* with what is perhaps the biggest and yet least talked about barrier to friendship: prejudice. While we now have educational and civil rights laws that work to prevent the outright exclusion of people with disabilities, we know we cannot legislate people's beliefs and feelings. We cannot negate the reality that, for many of us, our early lives were much closer to the first scenario than the second. And even if we were not given the message of "danger," we were still bombarded with television, fairy tales, movies and books that perpetuated the myth of disability as evil (Captain Hook in *Peter Pan*, 1951), pitiful (Tiny Tim in *A Christmas Carol*, 1953), ostracized (*To Kill A Mockingbird*, 1962), and institutionalized (*Rainman*, 1988).

We cannot and should not be faulted for having this core prejudice, it is a by-product of growing up in a world that still discriminates against people with disabilities. Not all of us were as fortunate as the family of the second scenario. And so when we talk about this prejudice, it should not make us feel guilt or shame. Instead it should encourage us to acknowledge this core inside us and vow to act against it all of the time.

Prejudice can serve as a barrier to friendship in countless ways. It is part of what makes dangerous assumptions possible. It can serve as a rationale for pull-outs and segregated classes. It is embedded into the promotion of a culture of "tolerance." And it is what we, inadvertently, teach other children when we perpetuate these barriers in schools.

Perhaps most dangerous is the fact that prejudice can cause us to doubt that a particular student could really have true friends. It can make us wonder if the best he can do is to have acquaintances, or people who care about him, or people who tolerate him. It can make us thrilled when someone acts nice to him or treats him in a friendly manner, because deep down inside we question if more is even possible. It can make us think that anyone who becomes his friend is doing so out of compassion or benevolence or to meet their own un-met needs. It makes us question why anyone would want to be his friend.

These beliefs serve as the ultimate barrier to friendship. They convey the message to the student and his classmates that friendship is beyond reach *because of who he is.*

Not long ago, toward the end of an all day workshop, I was asked the question, "Would *you* want to have a mentally retarded friend?" There was a gasp in the room as the audience leaned forward to hear what I was going to say. But I didn't know what to say. Not because answers to this obviously prejudiced question were not leaping to my lips. But because the person who asked the question was the mother of a 10 year old girl with Down syndrome. And what I think she was really asking was, "Do you truly believe anyone would want to be friends with my daughter?"

And so we know that prejudice is not unique to professionals. Parents who have children with disabilities were fed the same misinformation and narrow minded bigotry as the rest of us. And while their children challenge and change that core, the core can still exert influence. The mother who asked if I would want a "mentally retarded friend" still believed that one label defined her daughter and who she was as a person. And isn't that the definition of prejudice – beliefs and actions based on one characteristic to the exclusion of all others?

Our prejudice serves as a barrier to students being seen for their gifts, beauty, personalities, and thus keeps them waiting on the edge of the pool of potential friends.

 Friendship: What's the Real Problem? Revisited

For many years people have been working to figure out how exactly it is that we include students with disabilities in general education classes. Despite the commitment to getting this thing we call inclusion just right, many students are still pulled out of classes, still saddled with low expectations, and still spending the majority of their school day shadowed too closely by adults. Sure, they may spend most of their time in general education classes, but many of these students are still working outside of the curriculum and, at best, are only tolerated for who they are.

And so, to end our discussion of *Barriers*, we revisit the question posed at the start of this section: Friendship: What's the Real Problem?

Since each and every one of the barriers presented in this book runs counter to established educational best practices, the answer is clear. The real problem is that too many students are included in name only - they are in general education classes, but not true members - and this most definitely negatively impacts their academic, emotional, and social lives.

The solution? We need to bring best practices into every school and every classroom to ensure that all students are not simply "in" general education classes, but are valued as classmates, learners and yes, friends.

And now on to *Strategies*.

INTRODUCTION
TO STRATEGIES

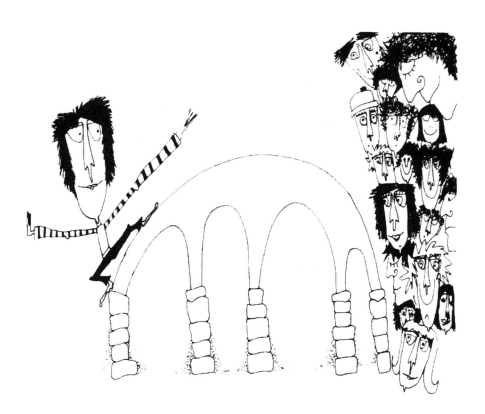

Whenever we begin a friendship workshop we point out that first we will teach about the barriers, followed by a discussion of strategies for supporting friendships. Inevitably, there are some in the audience who think, "Okay, I can doze through the barriers, but I will really start paying attention when they get to strategies."

We assume this might be the case with readers as well. And a few of you may have even skipped over the barriers section in order to jump right into strategies. But as we tell our audiences, that's not a good idea. Strategies are important and they can work, but they can also be frustrating. We have been using them for years, but often with no great outcomes. Why?

First, we believe that barriers are more powerful than strategies. When barriers keep the student out of the pool of potential friends, strategies have to work awfully hard to create true relationships. In other words, strategies have a tough time mitigating barriers. And since barriers are the real reason why so many students have no friends, simply implementing strategies will not get you to where you want to be.

Second, if we are not very careful, barriers can be embedded into the strategies we use. To illustrate what this can look like, we will use the case of Lily, a high school student who wants to join the Drama Club. It is an example of one of the most commonly used strategies around: *Join Join Join*, the strategy of supporting a student to join a club or group of people with similar interests or passions. Many of us have tried this strategy, but seldom do we get the kind of outcomes we are looking for. Let's look at some of the possible reasons why.

Barriers Inside of Strategies

To begin, think first about yourself. How do you decide which club or group or team you join? Chances are, it is based on your interests, passions, or desires. You join the book club because of your interest in reading. You join the peace and justice alliance because of your passion for social and economic justice issues. You join the aerobics class because of your desire to become more fit. Interests, passions, and desires. And once you are involved in those situations, you are surrounded by others who have similar interests. Which might mean you will meet someone you would like to get to know better.

But what would it be like if instead of the book club, you found yourself in the vintage car club? Not that there is anything wrong with vintage cars, it's just not what you are passionate about. Which probably means you will not be as outgoing, active, or enthusiastic as you might otherwise be. And therefore the likelihood of connecting with someone with similar interests decreases.

For many students with disabilities, the strategy of *Join Join Join* is sometimes used independent of the student's interests, passions or desires. Why? It could be a lack of awareness on the part of the adults, they may not think about or even know what the student is truly interested in. But more likely it is due to logistical considerations.

Consider: We know that Lily would love to join the Drama Club but the drama teacher is less than thrilled about having Lily in the club. And the special education teacher runs the Community Service Club so it would be much easier if Lily joined this club instead. And the paraprofessional who will be supporting Lily is very shy and would prefer to support Lily in something less outgoing, like the Sewing Club. And . . . you get the picture. Like finding yourself surrounded by Model Ts when you really want to read books, this is not the ideal situation for getting involved and meeting potential friends.

Are there other barriers that can work their way into strategies? You bet. Way too often we see one we call "Mainstreaming the Strategy."

Mainstreaming the Strategy

Let's go back to Lily and the Drama Club. We know that Lily loves the theater and is excited at being around others with similar passions. She will bring loads of enthusiasm to the club and is looking forward to sharing her acting skills with the other cast members. A seemingly perfect set-up for the *Join Join Join* strategy to work well.

But here is the hitch. The club meets every Tuesday and Thursday from 2:30 – 5:00 and, as the production nears completion, full rehearsals are scheduled for Wednesdays as well. But the paraprofessional who supports Lily is only able to work until 4:00, and never on Wednesdays. Therefore Lily misses the last hour of every meeting and does not attend Wednesday rehearsals. The cast often goes out for pizza after their meetings. But Lily's parents are not comfortable with Lily riding in another student's car, so unless the paraprofessional can drive, Lily does not join her cast mates. The production will be performed three nights in a row, but Lily will only participate in two of the performances, due to concerns that she will be too tired for school the next day. Lily is allowed to attend the closing night cast party but only for the first hour.

Will Lily make friends in this club? Who knows. But it seems less than a sure thing. She is not really one of the group, she is a part-timer, a visitor, a guest. Being mainstreamed into an activity comes with the same baggage that comes with being mainstreamed into a classroom. You may be "in" but you are not really "with." And that damages your chances of being part of that pool of potential friends.

Lack of Ongoing Support

The last barrier we often find embedded into strategies comes from the belief that once a student is in the right group, friendships will automatically bloom. And in some cases, this is absolutely true. But it is far more common to hear "I worked really hard to get her into this perfect club, and she loves it. But unless the group is meeting, she doesn't see or hear from any of the other members. I don't think she is going make any friends from this group."

This barrier happens when we believe that being in the right place is all the student needs. Yes, being in the right place is essential, but it often must be supplemented with the ongoing support. So, just as being in a general education classroom does not always lead to meaningful academic opportunities, being in a club does not always lead to reciprocal and meaningful friendships.

Values and Beliefs

Before we dive into the *Strategies*, we want to first share with you some of the key values and beliefs held by people who are successfully supporting friendships, and the guidelines they follow. If you read these and feel discomfort, we understand why. No one is perfect in these areas. We all struggle with the prejudice we were taught as children and how that impacts our lives today. Rest assured, you do not need to be perfect to do this job. But if you honestly feel that your values and beliefs are counter to those listed, perhaps the best decision you can make is to step aside and let someone else carry forward with these strategies, all the while learning more about the true gifts and abilities of those around you.

Subvert the Dominant Paradigm

The most important value for facilitating friendship is the unconditional belief that the student not only deserves a full and meaningful social life, but also that somebody would be extremely fortunate to have this student as a friend. Let us say that again. If you are going to support Jane to develop true friendships, you not only have to believe that Jane deserves these relationships, you also have to unconditionally believe that whoever gets to be friends with Jane is one incredibly lucky person.

We hope the paradigm shift is obvious. For too long, many of us who did the work of supporting students with disabilities had the mindset that the student with disabilities, Jane, would be so lucky if someone wanted to be her friend. Now there is nothing wrong with this per se, we are all lucky when we find that special someone who thinks we are terrific. But if we do not feel the same way about that person, then the deal is off. Unfortunately, for many students with disabilities the deal remained on, even if the relationship was a one way street.

So do you believe, deep down to your core, that the student you are supporting is worthy of true friendship? Do you believe that she would make somebody a wonderful friend? And that person would be extremely fortunate to have her in her life? If you can honestly answer all of these questions with an unqualified "Yes!" then you are well on your way to making this happen.

Be Like Water

Jeff Strully, well-known writer, teacher and parent, was once asked what to do when encountering an obstacle to reaching a dream. "Be like water," Jeff replied to the audience, and he was absolutely correct! What does water do when it gets to an obstacle? It goes over it. It goes under it. Around it. Through it. It finds the tiniest crack and seeps in. And sometimes it takes thousands of years but eventually wears it down and flows on through.

Being "like water" is another important guideline when supporting friendship. Believing that no matter the obstacle, friendship is too important to ever give up. And while we hope that it's not necessary to wait thousands of years to erode the barriers, we expect you will keep on keeping on until the water starts flowing through.

Intentionality

The late Marsha Forest coined the term "intentionality" as it relates to friendship. She made it very clear that we needed to *intentionally* - not forcing it, not believing it will happened with no effort, but *intentionally* - put time and spirit into supporting people to have the social lives they wanted. Anything less, she said, was unacceptable.

In our view, intentionality means that attention is paid to the reasons why friendship currently eludes this student (the barriers), and effort is made to avoid and overcome those barriers. But it also means that we cannot wait until all of the conditions are perfect, we need to act now to use strategies to support this student to make more connections, get more involved, meet more people, and make real friends. As Marsha taught us, we need to intentionally nurture the development of relationships.

Disregard the Social Dance

When thinking about supporting friendships, there is one question that gets asked far more often than all others: "How many times should my son extend invitations to classmates if he still has not received one in return?"

This is an important question and one that goes to the heart of what are considered social norms. For example, society says that if I invite you to dinner, I then await a return invitation from you. If this does not come, I may extend one more invitation but believe that the next step is yours. If you do not reciprocate, I am unlikely to extend a third invitation. I assume you are not interested (even though we had a lovely time together) and the relationship is over. This is the social dance we have been taught and have internalized oh-so-well.

When diving into the world of supporting friendships, it is important to recognize that the social dance can serve as an obstacle to possible relationships. The barriers that are placed in the paths of budding relationships between students with and without disabilities are still so great that following the rules of the social dance can result in a no-win situation. The playing field is not level, and so the rules themselves can become obstacles.

If there is one piece of advice we consistently get from people who are successfully supporting students to have the social lives they desire, it is this: Ask. Ask again. Ask one more time. And don't stop asking. As Marlyn Curtin once said, "How many times should Jocelyn have extended an invitation to get together with her friends? Once? Twice? Twenty times? What if we had stopped at five but the sixth one would have resulted in a return invitation? This is too important. It is an investment in the future. And so we never stop asking."

Just the Way You Are

Next we revisit a value mentioned in the *Introduction to Barriers*: a student does not need to change in order to have friends. As stated earlier, each of us are flawed human beings, and yet each of us have people in our lives who like and love us, just the way we are. For far too long, the onus for friendship – or the lack thereof – rested squarely on the shoulders of the student with disabilities. If only she could learn to talk more clearly, eat more neatly, walk more steadily. If only he could stop drooling, stop screaming, stop hitting. These beliefs led to students being squeezed into boxes that did not fit and were not comfortable. All the while being told that their chances for meaningful lives rested on their ability to conform.

Do you believe the student is worthy of friendship just the way she is?

This is Not a Disability Issue

While the focus of this book and the examples given involve students with labels of disabilities, it is important that we make it crystal clear that the issue of struggling with, wanting, and needing meaningful relationships in one's life is by no means limited to students with disabilities. In just about every school, there are students who suffer the pain and loneliness of exclusion. Their ways of expressing that pain are varied. Some students withdraw, others act out. Withdrawal can lead to further isolation, which at its most extreme can lead to suicide. Acting out can lead to further exclusion, which at its most extreme is prison or other forms of institutionalization.

Maslow's Hierarchy of Needs

(Before we begin our discussion of Maslow's Hierarchy of Needs, we want to thank Norman Kunc and Emma Van der Klift for brining the relevance of Maslow into this discussion of friendship. If you have not read any of Norman and Emma's writings on this, or any other subject, we encourage you to do so.)

Most of us have heard of Maslow's Hierarchy of Needs. Just about every high school and college psychology class teaches students about Abraham Maslow, who in 1943 postulated that the needs of human beings could be categorized into five hierarchical areas. The needs at the lower levels of the hierarchy must be met before a person can satisfy the needs at the higher levels. A representation of Maslow's Hierarchy is presented.

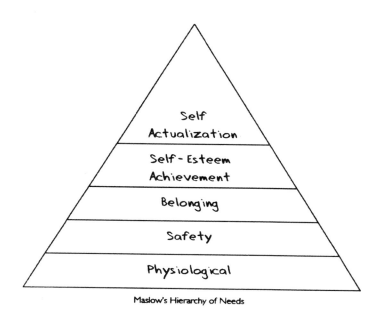

Maslow's Hierarchy of Needs

While there is much to learn from Maslow's Hierarchy of Needs, for the purpose of this discussion, we call your attention to the position of the "need to belong." As you can see, it is in the middle, after physiological and safety needs and before the need for self-esteem/achievement and self actualization. In other words, according to Maslow, the need to belong is a pre-requisite for self-esteem and achievement.

What does this teach us?

All people have the basic human need to belong. And the need to belong must be met before one can gain a sense of self- worth and achievement.

When we explain this during our workshops we see people in the audience nodding their heads in agreement. Of course we want kids to feel a part of the class or club or school. Of course this makes sense (the heads keep nodding), and of course we work hard to make it so.

But do we? Or do we say to students with disabilities the exact opposite? Do we send students the message that only once they achieve in special education science will they then be allowed in the regular science? Do we only "mainstream" students into those general education classes for which their achievement is good enough?

We put achievement ahead of belonging all the time. It is one of the protocols of our special education system.

So why do we challenge this? Are we asking you to think about this so that schools become kinder gentler places where everyone feels good? Yes. Are we asking you to think about this because attention to belonging increases the quality of student achievement? Yes. (In fact, one could argue that, according to Maslow, if we *really* want higher test scores we would be better off adding love to schools rather than remedial education.) But there is another reason we are asking you to pay very careful attention to the nurturing of belonging and community in schools - and it is a matter of life and death.

Think back twenty years and imagine you were asked to participate in a national conversation about the quality of education in our country. Regardless of our philosophical differences, it is probably safe to say that we all would have agreed on this one point: If there ever came a time when students began killing each other in schools, then we would *have* to change something and change it fast.

Unfortunately that time did come. All across the country, there are heartbreaking instances of students killing their classmates and themselves. And in nearly each instance, the reason for the violence is attributed to students' feelings of being bullied, left out, or harassed by peers. We have teenagers telling us, in the most dramatic ways, that they feel so alone that committing murder is somehow easier than carrying the burden of that pain.

Our national response? To hold schools more accountable for quality education by instituting more standardized tests.

One school district we know hired a full-time teacher to spend the school year teaching students how to do better on standardized tests. Imagine what that teacher could have done if his job was to spend a full year nurturing community and belonging in the school. And if he had done so, what would the tests score have looked like?

This is not a feel-good issue, this is the heart of the matter.

Maslow's hierarchy also makes it easier to understand why some students become members of gangs, behave promiscuously, or join groups of other disenfranchised youth. The need to belong is so great that people will seek out and find a community no matter the cost.

Belonging is not just a disability issue. We need to respond to the lack of belonging observed in individual students with a response that holds open its arms to the community building that is missing for everyone.

Circle of Courage

Our colleague Cathy Apfel has spent many years consulting with schools about students who have behaviors that are challenging to many people. It is striking how often Cathy uses the same strategy, no matter the situation. First, she observes in school and witnesses a day in the life of the student. Then she listens to the adults most involved with the student tell their perspectives. Then, she lays on the table the following diagram

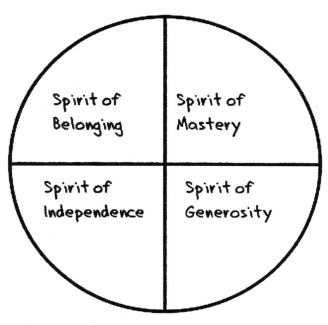

Circle of Courage
(Brendtro, Brokenleg, Van Bockern, 1990)

and asks the folks around the table to talk about the student in terms of each of the following: Generosity. Belonging. Independence. Mastery. Where in her life is the student able to give? Where does she belong? When is she trusted to be in charge of her decisions? At what is she so very talented?

Often the conversation stalls. Certainly the room is much quieter than it had been before. This is not what people were expecting. Where is the behavior modification plan? Where is the schedule of reinforcement?

What Cathy uses is called the "Circle of Courage," which comes from the book, *Reclaiming Youth at Risk: Our Hope for the Future* (1990) by Larry Brendtro, Martin Brokenleg, and Steven Van Bockern. It is based on Native American beliefs, and provides us even greater insight into the role that belonging plays in our human society.

The Circle of Courage suggests that all human beings have four basic needs - belonging, generosity, mastery, independence - which must be kept in balance in order for a person to be strong, healthy, pro-social and successful. Whenever any of the four are missing, less than desirable behaviors emerge. (Hard to believe? Have you ever eaten a quart of Ben and Jerry's ice cream when you were feeling heart-broken?) So while a team's goal to support a student's challenging behaviors may be worthy, the strategy to create a behavior modification plan is not. Instead, the plan must be to figure out how to make the student's life better - to balance the circle - and then watch what happens.

So what does the Circle of Courage tell us about friendship? It teaches, just as Maslow does, that belonging is not simply a desire, but a basic human need we all share. And friendship is not just a disability issue.

STRATEGIES:
WHAT TO DO

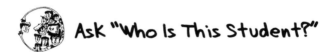 # Ask "Who Is This Student?"

No matter which strategies you use to help support a
student to have a full and meaningful social life, there is
one question that needs to be asked – and answered -
before any thing else is begun. The question: "Who is this
student?" is the first strategy to supporting friendships.

Now we don't mean "Who is this student?" from the
perspective of her IEP, permanent record, or professional
assessments. While those sources are certainly helpful in
some arenas, they do not contain the fountains of wisdom
we need to answer our question and really get to know
this student.

Perhaps the best way to help answer this question is to throw a few more questions into the mix:

Who is this student? What does she want? What are her interests? What are her dreams? What does she like? What does she dislike? What are her gifts and strengths? How does she spend her time? How does she want to spend her time? Who are the people in her life? Who is missing? What supports does she want and need?

And how do we answer these questions? By talking with, listening to, and carefully observing the student and the people who know her best.

It goes without saying that the student herself will be the greatest source of information. Figuring out the best way for the student to give you the answers may be challenging, but it is essential. Just taking the time to ask the questions is a great first step, but we must make sure the student's answers to these questions lead the way.

Observation is, of course, a wonderful way to learn more about the student. Observe the student in class, on the playground, in the cafeteria, at home. When is she most at ease? Who does she seem to like? What kinds of things does she enjoy the most?

Families know their children best and are invaluable resources when trying to understand a student's experiences, interests, and gifts. Families can provide information about the things their children do at home, which may translate into how a student can get involved in school. Families can also provide a historical perspective, such as which classmates a student has known for years and ways in which relationships were developed in earlier grades. And by families, we do not simply mean mothers and fathers. Sisters and brothers, too often ignored or marginalized by the educational process, can offer a wealth of information and ideas. Cousins and other extended family members may also be wonderful sources of suggestions.

We cannot say enough about how important it is to answer these questions by talking with classmates as well. Who knows more about what its like to be an 11 year old than another 11 year old? Classmates will be able to give us their opinions, their observations, and their advice, as well as the "real scoop" about what students their age do to make and enjoy friends. Students see things that adults often miss - or misread. Classmates are often masters at explaining challenging behaviors, which offers insight into what is missing (friends, communication, support) or overdone (hovering adults, support, modifications) in a student's life. Classmates care about friendship. They understand its importance and can see it as a priority over just about all else.

Educators are also crucial partners in answering these questions. Teachers and paraprofessionals not only see students daily, they also have great perspectives on the realities of relationships and community for specific age students. They can set up situations, in and out of the classroom, which give students opportunities to be together so you can observe what works and what does not. And previous teachers can offer wisdom gained from knowing the student in years past.

Additionally, neighbors, camp counselors, and coaches can be great sources of information and ideas.

When seeking the answers to these most important questions, it may be helpful to use one or more of the excellent person-centered planning tools that have been around for quite some time. MAPS and PATH (Falvey, Forest, Pearpoint, & Rosenberg, 1994) are two of the most common and most effective. We suggest you research these processes and use them to gain a greater understanding of "Who is this person?"

 ## Develop a Characteristic Pie

Now that you have begun the process of answering the most important question, you should determine the best way of sharing this information with other people in the student's life. While there are many ways to do this, we are partial to the one we call the *Characteristic Pie*, based on Norman Kunc's "disability spread."

The Characteristic Pie comes from the belief that each and every one of us is a collection of characteristics, some inherent, some developed, some acquired. And all of these characteristics combine to make us the unique and special people that we all are. As you can see from the example, the Characteristic Pie is a great way to develop a visual and easy to understand picture of the student, one which incorporates a variety of characteristics, not just one set of descriptors.

Characteristic Pie for Shaffer, age 17

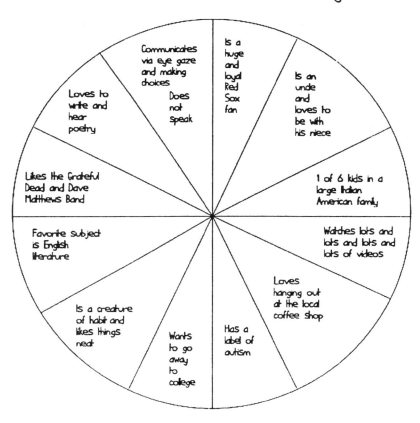

However, there are several guidelines to follow when developing a Characteristic Pie. The first involves the sources of information that inform the pie. No one person alone can create a pie (you cannot even make your own pie by yourself, there are things about you that others see that you may not even be aware of!). Luckily, the sources of information for the pie are the same sources for the answers to the *Most Important Question*.

The second guideline is called the no-jargon rule. Simply put, a Characteristic Pie should be free from professional jargon and should be able to be completely understood by anyone who reads it.

For example, in Shaffer's pie, one of the pieces says "watches lots and lots and lots of videos." Most anyone reading the pie will understand those words and be able to put them into a familiar context: *He loves videos. He watches a lot of them. Maybe he watches too many of them, like so many others his age. I wonder what kind of videos he loves.*

But imagine if we filled the pie with special education jargon. That one piece might have read "engages in perseverative behavior" or "has obsessive compulsive tendencies" or even "self-stims on familiar visual stimuli," none of which a person outside of special education would understand. And none of which are particularly useful in telling us who Shaffer is.

Why is this important? Because teachers and classmates and family members and friends will be reading this pie and will use it to help support Shaffer to meet and hang out with others who share his passions. And it is far more accurate and useful to describe what the student likes or does, rather than to prescribe a label to define it. Watches videos? Not only can we understand that, but we can probably find other kids his age who love to do the same thing!

Another guideline to follow is what Cathy Apfel calls the "Birthday Present Rule." When a Characteristic Pie is done correctly, anyone looking at it should be able to come up with an idea for a present to buy for the student's birthday. (Could you come up with a present to buy for Shaffer? Of course you could!) Why is this important? Again because it conveys information in useful terms that allow all readers to get a glimpse into Shaffer's true self.

Our fourth and final guideline simply relates to friendship. A good Characteristic Pie will help anyone who sees it to come up with a few beginning strategies to help this student connect more with others who share his interests. ("Shaffer, we will introduce you to other Deadheads, members of Red Sox Nation, and avid moviegoers.")

Every Inch My Son

One last note about the Characteristic Pie. Too often we fall into the trap of believing that one piece of the pie is more important than all others, especially when that piece holds a professional diagnosis. We begin to believe that all of a student's characteristics are products of their disability rather than a part of their personalities, interests, experiences, and upbringing. And then we start to make decisions based on "autism" or "cerebral palsy" rather than "love of music" or "mechanically inclined."

Once during a workshop, I asked a group of parents to make Characteristic Pies for their children. As they were nearing completion, I noticed one father was crying and I discretely asked him if he was okay. He stood and addressed the whole group. "While doing my son's pie, I suddenly realized he is exactly me at that age. We have the same interests, the same passions, the same quirks." He then explained that he was crying because, "My son has autism and I have become so conditioned to think of him *as* his autism. Because of that, I never realized how alike we are. Doing this pie made me realize that my son is so much more than 'autistic.' He is every inch my son."

 ## Join, Join, Join

Since we previously introduced the strategy of *Join Join Join*, you may already have a good understanding of the values and framework of this strategy. You know that if you are a passionate reader, joining the Book Club is a great way of meeting like-minded people. You also know the problems with joining the Ski Club if you despise winter sports. So let's dive right into ways of making this strategy work for the students you know and love.

As we discussed earlier, one of the ways students can meet other people who share interests and zeal is to join relevant clubs, teams, and other groups, both in and out of school. Just as it's important to be in all general education classes, it is similarly important to be involved in the same activities as one's classmates. Joining these groups is a great way to meet and hang out with others who share similar passions.

And no matter how obscure or unusual a person's interest, there will be others who share that passion. Dungeons and Dragons, magic cards, sheep shearing, Trekkies, paleontology, line dancing, karaoke, you name it, it's out there. In fact, we once heard a story of a man who collected air sirens. While you and I may think this is a very odd hobby indeed, he had just returned from the International Air Siren Convention in Moscow! Chances are no matter the passion of the student you are supporting, there is probably an international convention for those who share similar enthusiasm.

For this reason, it is important to support a student to find what is already out there for those who share his passions. These days, it seems as if there are almost endless numbers of groups and clubs, in and out of school. So please, take a good hard look at what is already out there, no need to create a new club or a "special" group. When you take that route, you not only waste precious time and resources, you also contribute to the notion that this student cannot participate in what already exists. And that communicates to classmates that this student is, at best, in the "kiddy pool" of potential friends.

What about the student whose interest is not common to others her age? Consider Molly, a middle school student who loves playing with dolls. She has several good friends who come over to her house on a regular basis and play with her dolls. When we asked these friends for an explanation, they let us in on a secret. They still love playing with dolls, but society has told them they are too old to have such interests. When they go to Molly's house, they are free to enjoy themselves in a authentic and expectation-free manner.

What a gift Molly has given to her friends!

But we also recognize that for some students their interest in "kid stuff" comes not from a genuine passion but from a lack of experience and exposure. A student may seem to love everything Barney, but is it his true desire or the expectations of others around him? If he is only given Barney videos to watch, Barney toys to play with, Barney t-shirts to wear, how do we know what he would do if given a true choice?

Deconstructing the Passion

But what about the student whose interest is truly out of the ordinary? (As if air sirens were ordinary!) For this we reflect on Samuel whose passion is fans. He loves to set up his fans to blow air across his face, to move things around in space, to create cross breezes in his room. He loves fans. Of course, because Samuel has a label of autism, it used to be said that he was "obsessed" with fans and with a behavior modification program his time his time with fans was limited ("If you behave, you can have time with your fans."). But now we recognize this to be a passion that Samuel has every right to enjoy.

But what about friends? If we started asking other students to tell us who else in the school is passionate about fans, we might draw a blank. So instead we "deconstructed" his passion and started talking about the elements of his interest to see who else might share some or all.

First we talked to the meteorology club and met students interested in wind and weather. They found Samuel's fascination with the movement of air quite ordinary. Then we talked to a Physics teacher who gave us the names of students who were working together to build ultra-light model planes. They were very interested to have someone with a knowledge of wind currents join them in their hobby. And we talked to students interested in mechanics, just to see if Samuel was interested in taking his passion with fans one step further. Were any of these groups called the Fan Club (pun intended)? No, but all shared something in common with Samuel's interests. And Samuel could be around others who appreciated his passion.

Learning to Be Together By Being Together

Joining clubs, groups, and teams based on shared interests and mutual participation not only locates students in the pool of potential (and like-minded) friends, but also opens up social opportunities they may never have known. When Ben entered high school, he joined the basketball team, which gave him the opportunity to meet many students who shared his passion for the sport. It was slow at first, but as the students began to see who Ben was and how much he had to offer, they developed a comfortable rapport. For these students, it was the first time they had gotten to know Ben without a paraprofessional by his side. They learned how he communicated, they figured out how to support him, they learned how much they all enjoyed each other's company. In other words, *they learned how to be together by being together.* And, not only did this group of students get together regularly for practice and games, they also hung out together in the hallways, at lunch, on the weekends and, of course, at victory parties! Ben never would have been a part of these opportunities if he had not followed his passion and joined the team.

 # Take Advantage of the Most Under-Utilized Resource: Students

True confession time. When I was a special educator, I regularly took two of my students to one of the big chain fast-food joints to teach them "appropriate restaurant behavior." The students were both in their early teens, I was in my thirties. *And* I was a vegetarian. Needless to say I was not exactly the best role model of appropriate teen behavior, especially in a place I had boycotted for years. As I was teaching my students to put their napkins on their laps, use manners, and "be neat," other teens their age were learning from each other important skills such as splitting one small order of fries six ways, how to squirt ketchup packets across the room, and where the cute boys hung out.

OK, maybe this is a slightly exaggerated example (I don't think I made my students put their napkins on their laps!), but only slightly. And the point remains true - no adult can really know what it is like to be a child, a teenager, or a young adult. We can *remember* what it was like when we were that age, but we cannot put ourselves into the sneakers of a young person today. And for that reason, we are at a definite disadvantage when we work on supporting friendships.

However, the solution to this problem is close at hand. Everyday we are surrounded by students who are more than willing to give us their twenty-five cents worth on what it's like to be a kid today, if only we would ask them.

That is why the strategy of talking to students is one of the most useful, and often the easiest to put into place. We do not need to wonder, we only need to take advantage of the precious but severely under-utilized resources that are all around us.

By the way, some teams feel so strongly about the need for regular student input that they never have an IEP or a major planning meeting without including one or two same age classmates to participate - alongside the student of course!

The Knack of Talking with Kids

When we first started talking to young people about their ideas and suggestions around friendships, we quickly learned there is a knack to talking with students. Young people, like many of us, are masters at saying what they think adults want to hear. And so when we entered into conversation wearing our "authority figure" hats, all we got were platitudes and party-lines (one time we actually got a recital of the school's mission statement). But when we let our guard down, honestly asking for advice and admitting that without their perspective we could not succeed, the floodgates opened. We were amazed by how generous the students were with their suggestions and how honest they were with their ideas. We were in business!

So if you can temporarily lose your teacher or parent hat, we offer you some guidelines and strategies for talking with students. But, if you are not comfortable taking off that hat, we suggest you find someone else to do the talking. Students of all ages are quick to notice when someone is uneasy or disingenuous with them, and, from our experience, they will be far less willing to give you the real story.

Ask Students: General Fact Finding

We have said it before: students can give us the full scoop on many of our questions. What does friendship typically look like for an eight year old? What do 7th graders do with their friends? What's out there for a 15 year old with a passion for graphic design? What's it like in the cafeteria? The playground? The halls? When do friends get to see each other in school? How important are extracurricular activities? What about summers? Authentic answers to these questions guide us as we support students to develop the social life they want and deserve.

These kinds of questions are not necessarily student-specific and can be asked to a diverse group of young people. We consider this research or fact-finding, and it gives us a starting point when thinking about how to facilitate friendships in general.

One note: Please do not assume you know the answers to these questions just because you work in a school. We are constantly surprised with students' answers to these questions and learn something new every time we ask them.

Ask Students: Student-Specific

Students are also an important source of information for our student-specific questions. Perhaps we are brainstorming ideas for supporting Jorma's social life. If we want to know if Jorma is even in the pool of potential friends, we need to speak with some of his classmates and get their perspectives on his social status in the classroom. If we want to see how he can connect with others who share his love of videogames, we need to ask a small but diverse group of classmates to tell us who in the classroom and school also love video games. These students can tell us who Jorma likes and who likes him and they can give us suggestions on how to nourish those sparks. They can tell us everything from what others in his class do after school to how Jorma can better participate in cooperative learning groups. These students can be asked to give us their honest appraisals on how Jorma's paraprofessional is viewed by classmates, concerns students have about Jorma's challenging behaviors, and questions about Jorma's communication system. They can also be asked for their opinions on how to make these supports more effective and inclusive.

Is Jorma involved in these conversations with his classmates? Of course, *unless* he expresses a clear preference not to be.

It is hard not to write pages and pages of caution about this strategy. Done correctly, it is an extraordinary way of gaining information to support friendship. Done incorrectly, it is possible to alienate classmates, stigmatize Jorma, and generally portray students with disabilities as in need of charity and compassion, rather than worthy of friendship and love. So, not only do you have to leave your authority figure hat at home, you also need to leave behind any remnants of benevolence or pity you may carry for Jorma or students with disabilities in general. If you cannot, find someone else to do this.

Advisory Boards

One way to have regular and open conversations with a familiar group of students is to develop an "advisory board" or a group of students who advise *you* on how to best support a specific student. This group of students can meet on a regular basis to identify social events, discuss happenings in a student's life, and problem-solve around important issues. Advisory boards are there to present this wealth of information to *you*, not the student you are supporting. Of course the student is a part of this process, unless she or he prefers not to be.

Some people say that having an adult or two on the advisory board enhances its efficacy by bringing even more information and experience into the group. While we have no strong objections to this twist, we do advise that caution be exercised to prevent the adult voices from overpowering the students. Many young people who are involved in intergenerational groups express frustration at finding their right to be heard challenged by the adults' disapproval or desire for control.

One last point. It is important to recognize the differences between an advisory board and a "circle of friends." The focus of the advisory board is on the information classmates can provide to you, thus the term *advisory* board. Advisory board members are not enlisted to become the student's friend or to even engage in social activities with the student. In other words, when gathering a group of classmates to form an advisory board, the question is not "Who wants to be Isaiah's friend?" but instead "Who would be willing to help me better support Isaiah to have the social life he desires?"

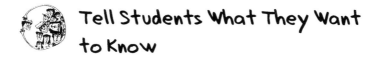 ## Tell Students What They Want to Know

In addition to asking for information and advice from students, it is also important to openly and honestly answer their questions and concerns. What information you provide, and how and when you provide it is key to this strategy's success.

Consider this: You and I meet at a party and we hit it off right away. After about 10 minutes of small talk, I start to tell you about my difficult childhood, my recent surgery (I even show you my scar!) and how I am flat broke. And by the way, "Can you lend me $500?"

Or this: Your five year old asks you how babies get here and you begin to launch into a discussion of sperm and egg, fertilization and gestation. Just as you are about to get into the delicacies of the birth canal, your daughter screws up her face and says, "Mommy, I meant if you don't have a car seat, how would the baby get home from the hospital?"

Or how about this one: Ellie and Lindsay are starting to develop a budding friendship. Lindsay invites Ellie over for dinner but before Ellie's mom agrees, she talks to Lindsay about Ellie's medication (even though she only takes them in the morning), how to change her diapers (even though she will not need a change during dinner) and her history of seizures (even though she has not had one in years).

Overwhelmed, Lindsay sighs and says never mind, she will just see Ellie at school the next day.

Only one of these stories is true (the middle one – did you guess?), but unfortunately the third one is true in spirit. Far too often we hear variations of the Ellie/Lindsay story, with similar outcomes. It is a perfect example of how too much unnecessary information, given at inappropriate times, can scare away a new friend.

Giving Useful and Necessary Information

Giving students the information they need and want to know is an effective, but delicate, strategy. Does a student need to know her new friend's complete medical diagnosis or does she need to know how to best support her to communicate? Does she need to know her friend's list of medications or just what foods she is allergic to? Is the textbook definition of autism required or rather an explanation of why her new friend does not make eye contact? The information we give students should be what is useful and necessary for friendships to bloom.

So how are you going to give new or potential friends necessary and useful information?

First, we need to realize that what we think is necessary and useful is not always in sync with what students think is necessary and useful. For that reason, we ask students two questions: "What do you want to know?" and "What do you need from us to allow this friendship to blossom?"

"What do you want to know?" is a pretty straightforward question, but it takes a good ear to recognize what students are really asking. Just like the five year old asking about babies, we need to listen to what the student really wants to know. If you hear "What's wrong with him?" you might realize this is a question asking why Roberto screams when he hears a loud noise. The question of "How come he can't talk?" is a good opportunity to discuss the variety of ways we all communicate and to point out the numerous ways Roberto tells us what he wants and knows. In other words, being a good listener is a key to being a good answerer.

The second question we ask students is: "What do you need from us to allow this friendship to blossom?" This question respects the needs of students to develop ways, at a comfortable pace, in which they can and will support their new friend. For example, John might say he initially needs an adult to be around in case Martin needs to move out of his wheelchair. We need to respect these needs as new relationships begin to develop.

Before we move on, let's quickly revisit the first (fictional) example, the one where I ask to borrow money. Demanding too much too soon of a new friend is a recipe for disaster. Chances are that budding relationships will die on the vine once it is clear that one party is asking for much more than the other party can or is willing to provide.

For too many students with disabilities, the demands that get placed on their new or potential friends are huge and often unreasonable. Just as you should not be expected to lend me money right away, a potential friend should not be expected to get "med certified" or provide bathroom support before getting a chance to see if the sparks will turn into a flame. We need to ask students what they need from us and then deliver.

A Word About Labels

A quick note about labels. Whenever anyone wonders about using words such as "autism" or "Down syndrome" with students, I always tell them the same story. In the mid '60's a new family moved into our neighborhood. I was eight years old and very excited to meet the new neighbors - until I heard my parents talking. When describing the family, my mother whispered, "They are Negroes." (Apologies for the word, it was 1965 and that was still commonly used by mainstream Americans.) But it was not the word that stuck in my mind, it was the fact that my mother had whispered it. That whisper gave me the impression there was something wrong with the word, and consequently with the new neighbors.

When we whisper something, literally or figuratively, we send a very strong message about its value and desirability. If we never use the word "autism" or use it only in the context of a stereotype or medical diagnosis, we run the risk of conveying to students that it is something negative and undesirable.

However, we also cannot give too much weight to these words. When answering a classmate's question "Why doesn't Leslie look at me when we're talking?" we think it is completely appropriate to explain that Leslie has a label of autism and lots of people with autism say that making eye contact is a painful or difficult thing to do. But it's equally important to go on to discuss all of the ways Leslie shows she is listening, and how we can let Leslie know this is understood. We believe this way of conveying information respects the label as one (and only one) of Leslie's characteristics, but gives it no more importance than it deserves.

A Word about Classroom Presentations

It hopefully goes without saying that we are not advocating giving students the information they want and need via whole class presentations. Nor are we suggesting using "handicap awareness" programs or demonstrations. It is our belief that these means of conveying information run counter to the messages we want students to receive. We do not want Meg's 5th grade class to think they know about Meg because they heard a presentation about Down syndrome. We do not want Juan's 8th grade classmates to believe they know him better because they did a simulation exercise on being blind. We want to give the people in Meg's life information about her so they can get to better know her as a person and a potential friend. We want Juan's classmates to know that they can and should ask questions and can interact with Juan as they would with anyone else. And so we answer questions as they arise, individually or in very small groups, and always within the context of real life experiences.

 ## Find an Insider

When I first met 25 year old Cary, he was new to the city and feeling more than a bit isolated. When I asked him what kind of things he was interested in, he responded that as a child he had always loved church. And so I invited him to come with me to the church I attended. Sure I could have just pointed him toward the dozens of churches in the area, even offered him a ride, but I knew the benefits of being invited into a new group by someone who is already a member. And so on Sunday, we went to church together. There I introduced Cary to various members and helped him follow the traditions. When, during the service, one of the members rose to make an announcement about the weekly drum circle, Cary's eyes lit up. After service I asked if he would like me to introduce him to this member. The result? Cary wants to continue to attend church, has a lunch date with the minister, and plans to attend the drum circle next week. Not bad for a few hours on a Sunday.

Would these outcomes have been the same if Cary had attended this church on his own? Or if I had gone with him to a different church, one where we were both strangers? Maybe, maybe not. But in the art of supporting friendship, we have learned that it is better to be invited in by an insider than taken in by an outsider.

Let us say that again: When entering a new situation, it is tremendously advantageous to be brought in, introduced, and supported by an insider, someone who is already a part of the group.

This has great implications for supporting students to join and participate in opportunities of their choosing. Imagine you are supporting Alex, a high schooler who is interested in becoming a part of the wrestling team. Now also imagine you know nothing about wrestling, and in fact are pretty uninterested in the sport. How awkward would it be for you to accompany Alex to the wrestling team meeting, trying to introduce him to people you do not know, attempting to support him to understand the culture and routine when you yourself are uninformed? How much better would it be to have an insider, a member of the wrestling team, bring Alex into the group? In much the same way I was able to support Cary in church, this insider would be able to help Alex meet the players, get a handle on the expectations, and more easily suggest a role for Alex on the team.

So does this mean you can only support students who share your interests and desires? Of course not. But part of supporting friendship is figuring out how to find an insider right from the start.

One way to do this is to utilize the concept of "advisory boards." Because an advisory board is a group of students who offer guidance to you as you intentionally support relationships, it is a perfect way to help you find an insider.

Let's go back to Alex. One way to find an insider is to ask some questions of the advisory board: "Alex wants to join the wrestling team. Who knows someone on the wrestling team? Does that person already know Alex? If not, how can we help that person get to know Alex (better)? What does that person need to become the insider who brings Alex into the wrestling team?"

Easiest would be if someone on the advisory board is a wrestler himself. But more commonly, the process begins with "my sister's boyfriend's best friend's next door neighbor is on the wrestling team," and leads to brainstorming ways to get this person to get to know Alex and become the insider.

If you are not convinced of the need for this process, which does take time and creativity, think about yourself for a moment. If you moved into a new town, wouldn't it be nice to have an insider show you around?

 **Enlist a Bridge Builder**

The strategy of *Finding an Insider* is an effective way of helping a student enter into a group of students. We also offer the strategy of finding a *Bridge Builder* as a way of supporting a student to become more involved with the greater social structure of her school or community. A bridge builder could certainly be the insider but more likely she is the person who finds the insider.

There are many ways to develop the strategy of bridge building:

Using her respite money, the parent of a 4th grader hired a high school student who excelled in soccer to be a community bridge builder for her son. The high school student took the boy, who also loved soccer, to places where others interested in the sport spent their time. He served as both mentor and bridge builder, supporting the boy to get more involved with the sport and the players.

Using a small state grant, a high school hired a new college graduate to serve as a bridge between one student and the greater school community. She talked to students to find out what they did after school, where they hung out, and how to best help this one student become better connected to his classmates.

Another school, piggybacking on the previous example, hired a high school senior to serve as a bridge builder for one student. This senior was not hired to be the student's friend (remember that barrier?) but instead to be the connector between the student and his classmates. The bridge builder found out what was happening on weekends and after-school and supported the student to get more involved.

In these examples, the bridge builder serves the critical role of connecter, but the role can be so much more. For some students, a bridge builder can be the person who helps interpret or explain behaviors that may be confusing to classmates. When left unexplained, actions such as avoiding eye contact or repeating phrases may cause classmates to believe the student is uninterested in or unable to have a relationship. We know that this is clearly not the case, but classmates may be left to wonder. The bridge builder can explain the meaning behind such actions and ensure that the student is introduced as a competent person with a unique personality and gifts to offer.

A bridge builder does not need to be a person hired specifically for this role, although our experience tells us this is helpful. But whoever the bridge builder, he or she must have a clear set of beliefs about the abilities and giftedness of all students. And while paraprofessionals may indeed help build some bridges for students, the role of the bridge builder and the role of the paraprofessional are distinct and separate.

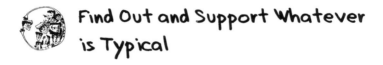

Find Out and Support Whatever is Typical

For a few years, I facilitated a monthly gathering of people interested in supporting Andrea to have the kind of social life she wanted and deserved. The meetings were always a joy, as this team would stop at nothing to help Andrea get what she wanted. I arrived late to one meeting and walked into a lively discussion about the best ways to start "Andrea's Quilting Club." We all knew that Andrea loved to sew and believed she would enjoy getting together with others to sew and quilt. When I arrived, team members were busy talking about how to find donated sewing machines, fabric, and a place to meet. Needless to say the enthusiasm was great and the creative ideas were flying. A "to do list" was already overflowing with the many tasks needed to get this idea up and running.

As a latecomer to the meeting, I was struck by two things. First the energy and enthusiasm of the team (hooray!) and second that I had just driven past the local headquarters for Caring Quilts, a longstanding quilting club that gathered weekly to make quilts for babies born with HIV. This group was housed in the community center, had numerous sewing machines, a seemingly endless supply of fabric, and lots of members. And while I did not want to dampen the enthusiasm of Andrea's team, I knew I had to ask: Did they really want to start something new when almost exactly what they were looking for already existed? Luckily this was not only a creative team but a practical one as well. They quickly shifted their focus and soon their much-shortened "to do list" contained contacting Caring Quilts, finding an insider, and enrolling Andrea in the club.

One of the basic strategies for supporting relationships starts with this principle: Before creating something from scratch, first find out what's already out there.
This strategy has numerous benefits. First, it saves time. For Andrea and her team to create a new club, it would

have taken weeks to gather the necessary materials, space, and people to make it a reality. Instead, by taking advantage of an existing opportunity, their time and energy was better spent on creating the necessary supports for Andrea's successful participation. A second benefit of this strategy is that it allows the student to be where people with shared passions naturally gather. Andrea does not need to bring together people who love to quilt, she can go to where they already congregate. A third benefit is the shift in the status quo that can result from a new member. When Andrea, who is not able to see colors and details, joined the quilting club, she began to use a wide variety of textures and weave to create her quilts. As a result, other members began to experiment with textures and soon babies around the region were getting quilts that were tactilely interesting and diverse. Eventually the status quo of what made a beautiful baby quilt was changed forever.

A Special Note To Educators

One of the wonderful things about teachers is that they are famous for being able to create something out of very little (look what they do with their small classroom budgets each year!). However, we hope that the above example will encourage teachers to use their remarkable creativity to research what already exists for students who love videos or animals or badminton or travel, rather than creating a new club or group. We have seen, all too often, that these well-intentioned creations become "special-ed clubs" and draw primarily students with disabilities, with a few student-helpers along for the ride.

 # Use Get Acquainted Activities

Every year, classroom teachers face a brand new group of students with whom they will spend 10 months creating a community of learners. There are countless numbers of "first day of school" and "get-to-know-each-other" activities available in stores and on the web to help teachers get off on the right foot. (Google "first day of school activities" and you will be overwhelmed with tens of thousand of hits.) Needless to say, the education field takes seriously the many ways in which teachers can help students learn about themselves and their new classmates at the beginning of each school year.

An intriguing strategy to support relationships (and one that is fairly easy to use) is to take advantage of this vast array of resources to specifically facilitate one student's connections with his classmates. Let's take one example.

A get acquainted activity frequently used in schools is the "Me Box." A teacher instructs each student in the class to come to school with a shoebox filled with seven or eight things which represent who they are. Students commonly fill their boxes with photographs, sports equipment, favorite music, hobbies, vacation memorabilia; whatever represents their personalities, interests, experiences. In class, students are paired to share their boxes, and the pairing continues for several days, with students eventually getting into groups of four and then eight. In the end, every student has shared his or her box with every other student. Teachers and students alike report this to be a bonding experience that allows all students to get to know each other and show off their unique personalities, as well as learn about shared interests and passions.

It is probably not difficult to see how this common class activity can be used as a friendship strategy. Teachers can introduce these kinds of activities at any point in the school year, and while they may do it to directly benefit one student, chances are many others will benefit as well. Also, because activities such as "Me Boxes" are not solely language-based, they are great supports for students who do not speak or speak easily.

A note about older students: It was traditionally believed that activities such as "Me Boxes" were only appropriate for elementary age students and secondary school students were too mature for those kind of activities. Two things have changed people's minds. First, teachers who used "Me Boxes" and similar activities with students in middle and high school noted the overwhelming success of such activities. Students valued the opportunities to define who they were on their own terms, not based on old assumptions or biases. Students appreciated the chances to discover the many ways they were both the same and different from their classmates. New friendships were often forged as a result of this new information.

The second realization came from programs and strategies that support the integration of exchange students into American high schools. Many of these exchange programs have get-acquainted type activities built into their curriculum, designed to support students not familiar with the school culture or not well-versed in the language to become more engaged with the school community. Some of these strategies involve peer guides (bridge builders) and non-language based activities to discover shared interests.

 ## Pay Attention to the Sparks and Natural Connections

Ah, love. Is it chemistry? Magic? Circumstance? Does anyone really know or can we only hope that when the sparks start to fly we are smart enough to pay attention?

Ah, friendship. Is it chemistry? Magic? Circumstance? Does anyone really know or can we only hope that when the sparks start to fly we are smart enough to pay attention?

Yes, we did write those words twice. Intentionally. For love and friendship have so much in common, especially the sparks. And when engaged in the process of supporting friendships, an important strategy is to pay close attention to any sparks that may be starting to fly between students.

Let's look at a painfully obvious example of how important it is to pay attention to the sparks.

In order to make sure Hannah had someone to eat lunch with, her teacher developed a rotating "cafeteria buddy" list to determine each day who would sit with Hannah in the cafeteria. Luckily, after a few weeks, an observant lunchroom assistant noticed that Hannah only seemed to enjoy lunch on the days Latisha was assigned to be her "buddy." The assistant suggested to the team that perhaps Hannah did not need - or want - a rotating lunch buddy, but instead wanted to nourish her budding friendship with Latisha. As the team met, one by one they told stories of how the girls sought each other out in groups, sat together when it was free time, gravitated toward each other on the playground. In other words, stories of the sparks that were starting to fly. When Latisha was asked about this, she said that she liked Hannah and really wanted to eat lunch with her every day. When asked why she didn't, this honest and trusting young girl replied that she thought she was only allowed to do so on the day she was assigned. The team promptly ripped up the chart (bravo!) and decided that they would work to support this budding relationship between the two girls.

Many people believe that the greatest barrier to friendship is missed opportunity. They say that we adults are too busy doing this and that to see what is right in front of our eyes – the clear signals that two students might have a potential relationship brewing. And so we suggest two strategies.

First, open your eyes a little wider to the sparks. Commit yourself to taking the time to observe what is happening between the student you are supporting and others in his life. Is there one student with whom he seems to have a natural affinity? Is there a student who has a natural affinity for him? Does someone make him brighten? Are there looks exchanged? Sparks flying?

Secondly, pay attention to the natural opportunities for relationships to develop. Are two students both wearing

Spearhead concert t-shirts? Did you overhear one student talking about a movie that you know is a favorite of the student you are supporting? How do you notice these commonalities and use them to create a bridge between students?

There is never any guarantee that sparks will fly and love or friendship will bloom. But we can increase the odds by seeing what is often right in front of us, if only we take the time to pay attention.

 **Avoid Clusters**

An important strategy to keep in mind when working to support relationships is to keep your focus on one student at a time. While it might be tempting to think, "Well I have two students, both of whom are interested in sports, I could support both of them to become members of the field hockey team," there is great danger in this approach. If two students, both of whom have disabilities and both of whom are supported by you, join the field hockey team, it is extremely likely that they will be seen as a pair – an already established group – and not as unique individuals. And true integration, to say nothing of friendships, is less likely. Is this fair? Probably not, but it is true. Experience shows that teammates, as well as coaches, will see these two students as a group unto themselves and will be less likely to truly include them into the workings of the team.

This is not to say you cannot successfully work on supporting more than one student at a time to develop the kind of relationships they want and deserve. It is just important to consider each student uniquely, as his or her own person, and not grouped with others you support.

 **Be Visible**

How do any of us meet the people who eventually become our friends? It probably goes without saying that the odds increase the more people we are around. We have to come into contact with lots of people to find the ones with whom we share interests and truly click.

Maybe it goes something like this: You see and are seen by thousands of people. You are around hundreds of people on some sort of regular basis. You make a connection with scores. You really get to know dozens. You make a special bond with one or two. From thousands to someone special - if you are lucky.

For this reason, a valuable way to support students to develop relationships is called the *Be Visible* strategy. Cassady is a great example of this.

Cassady is in 8th grade in her neighborhood school. She attends all general education classes, is a member of several extracurricular clubs, and goes to most of the school dances, sporting events, and concerts. She is a member of the community soccer league and her church's youth group. She and her younger sister walk their dog through the neighborhood each evening and she eats out often with her family. Needless to say, she is well-known throughout her community.

Will all of this visibility guarantee that Cassady will make some great friends? Of course not, but it certainly increases the odds. Is all of this visibility enough? Probably not, but as one strategy, it certainly makes a lot of sense.

One way to use this strategy is to make sure the students you support are full and valued members of general education classes in their neighborhood schools (the definition of inclusion!). As social institutions, schools have the opportunity – and the obligation – to not simply mimic society but to better it. By ensuring all students are fully included, you are helping them to increase their visibility and subsequently make the world a better place.

Another way to support this strategy is to help students, families, schools, and communities understand the importance of visibility. Remind them that the history of people with disabilities is filled with segregation, isolation, institutionalization, and loneliness. Ask them to think back to their childhoods – did they ever see people who had disabilities? Where were they? Remind them that although times have changed and people with disabilities are taking their rightful places in society, old assumptions and prejudices are still around. And one way to counter these biases is to support students with disabilities to be fully visible and valued members of their schools and communities. We can support each student to be everywhere and do everything they want – play outside, go to the movies, eat out, have sleepovers, attend community events, date, support local teams, attend college, work, join leagues and clubs. Be visible! Show the world that everyone belongs and deserves a full life. For the more visible you are, the more difficult it is for someone to deny you the opportunity to really live!

So What about Community Based Instruction?

Some may read these suggestions about visibility and think, "Great! We have this covered. We take our students out in the community during the school day to shop at the mall, eat at a restaurant, ride the bus..."

Wait! Please wait. Is this *really* what we are talking about?

Community-based instruction has been around for quite some time. And in the beginning it made perfect sense. When students with disabilities were relegated to segregated schools and classrooms, it was far better for students to learn *in the community* rather than in special education classrooms. If you were going to teach a student to ride a bus, better it be a real bus than a simulated bus made of cardboard boxes and classroom chairs. (Yes this is a real example. "Back in the day" many special education classes created pseudo bus stops, grocery stores, and apartments in their classroom to "teach" students those skills.)

But we are no longer in those days. We have recognized the importance of students with disabilities being full-time members of general education classes, learning skills and knowledge alongside their peers. And if a student needs to learn how to ride a bus, shop in a store, cash a check? Well those things can be taught at times when other students are also engaged in those activities – after school, weekends, evenings, summers, after graduation.

So does community-based instruction support the strategy of *Be Visible*? Yes, if it happens during times when the community is filled with students, but most definitely not if it is done during the school day. For how can you "be visible" if you are removed from the very place all others your age are spending their days?

Real or Forced Choices?

This may be a good time to discuss our beliefs about two people with disabilities becoming friends with one another. We are often asked the question "What about two students from a self-contained special education classroom who become great friends?" This question is generally expressed as a challenge to our commitment to full inclusion with the person posing the question rejecting the notion that inclusion and visibility are necessary conditions for the development of relationships.

First, let us make it clear that we do not believe anyone has the right to say that two people with disabilities should not be friends with one another. We know that love and friendship are magical and we honor all relationships that are meaningful to each partner.

That said, we also believe that it is essential not to limit anyone's choices or life experiences. By limiting opportunities, we eliminate options and choices, offering "forced choices" instead of real ones.

The notion of "forced choices" comes to bear when we are talking about a student whose daily life involves only a small group of people. While we honor all relationships, we must honestly question whether these relationships are the result of informed or forced choices. If I am around only ten other people, then I only have a pool of ten potential friends. And while I may make a friend, I am denied the opportunity to see who else is out there.

Bottom line? We have the obligation to support students with disabilities to be fully visible and valued members of their schools and communities. Then, and only then, will we know that their relationships truly come from choice.

 **Identify The Non - Negotiables**

In the *Barriers* section we used the term "non-negotiable," defined by Jeff Strully as those things on which you are not able to bend. They are what they are. Period.

To illustrate: Mina was a high school junior and starting to get friendly with two girls from school. Sparks were flying and real friendships were starting to bloom – *in* school. But whenever Mina received an invitation to get together after school, she said no. It didn't matter if it was an invitation to the movies, a dance, or a party, all were turned down. Why? If you asked Mina's friends, they assumed Mina was not really interested in them, or her mother did not trust or like them. Whatever the reason, all they knew is that all of their attempts were thwarted. And so after a while, they stopped trying. And soon their friendship began to fade.

When we first heard this story, we were baffled. We had seen Mina and these girls together and it was obvious they all liked each other. We had spoken to Mina's mom who was thrilled that her daughter had made friends with such wonderful girls. So why were all invitations rebuffed?

The answer to this question came out of the blue. When chatting one day, Mina's mother mentioned that Mina went to bed every night at 7:00 pm. Not because she was tired, but because the only person in the household who could lift her into bed, left for work at that time. If he did not get Mina into bed, she would have to stay in her wheelchair until he returned home in the early morning. This was a schedule the family had worked out years ago, and it was not going to change.

It suddenly became clear. Invitations were not refused because of personality or interest, they were refused because of a non-negotiable - the 7:00 pm bedtime!

An important strategy for supporting friendships is to encourage the open and honest discussion of everyone's non-negotiables. Kept secret, they create mistrust and uncertainty. Out in the open they remove barriers and create opportunities.

When Mina and her mother finally told the girls the reason for rejecting their invitations, it eased their concerns. Okay, Mina could not hang out in the evenings, but what about directly after school? And weekends? As long as she was home before 7:00, they could enjoy each other's company and rekindle their budding friendship.

An epilogue to this story. By finally understanding this non-negotiable, the school and family began to discuss ways to support Mina at bedtime. Ideas ranged from arranging for a home health care provider to help Mina get into bed, to purchasing a lift to move Mina from her chair into her bed. Once the conversation began, the ideas flowed. And who knows? Maybe someday the 7:00 pm bedtime will no longer be a non-negotiable.

Write Friendship into the IEP

Many professionals and families have love-hate relationships with IEPs (Individualized Educational Plans). Every year teams struggle with how to write them to meaningfully express the true nature of the abilities and support needs of their students. And some teams have been trying to figure out if and how the IEP can include friendship.

But what does including friendship into the IEP look like? Will we begin to see IEPs that state "Esther will have three friends, 80% of the time, on two consecutive data days"?

Of course not (although that would make for some interesting data collection!!). What we do see written into the IEP are things such as:

- friendship development written into the supports and services

- an entire IEP written in ways that ensure true inclusion

- person-centered goals that focus on the student's strengths and learning style

- a Characteristic Pie as part of the student profile

- many goals and objectives written around small group work and cooperative learning

- objectives for one or two "get acquainted" activities

- objectives starting with phrases such as "working with a small group of classmates" or "working with a student of her choosing"

- strategies on how to identify, avoid and remove barriers written into the supports section

Writing friendship into a student's IEP is a strong way to convey its importance. However, many teams are cautious of this strategy. Some worry that it will take the focus away from academic goals, although the interdependence between academics and friendship are clearly expressed in the examples above. Some worry that by putting friendship into the IEP, the sole responsibility for a student's social success will rest with the school, however we know that it is only with true collaboration between family and school that all aspects of a student's education will be maximized. Some are concerned that friendship is not a measurable concept thus there is no true way of determining success. We suggest that by improving our observational skills as well as our interviewing skills we can begin to identity what we would see and hear if friendship was becoming a reality.

 ## Plan Cooperative Experiences for All Students

Experiential learning and cooperative experiences such as Outward Bound, ROPES courses, and environmental camps are designed to teach students to appreciate their own abilities and the gifts and abilities of others. They aim to challenge students to get out of their comfort zones and try new things, to work together to solve problems, and to confront their own fears. Schools offer these opportunities in order to teach students respect for themselves, their surroundings, and their fellow students. Although it is understandable to wonder how to make these opportunities possible and positive for all students, our experience shows us that the rewards of having everyone participate far outweigh the challenges.

Imagine the benefits of this decision. Each year 6th grade
students from West Middle School attend a week-long
environmental camp. Although the team struggled with
how to make this experience work for Mohammed, who
needs a variety of support to get through his day, they
were committed to his participation in all aspects of the
week, including living in the cabin, hiking up Mt. Blue,
doing camp chores, and testing his resolve on the ROPES
course. As a result, students developed a respect and
appreciation for one another, and the relationships made
that week were sustained throughout the school year.

If we believe these experiences are worthwhile, then to
exclude even one student is antithetical to the values and
desired outcomes. The experiences which provide all
students the opportunity to live, work, and play together
in challenging and interdependent ways can result in the
development of long-lasting relationships, based on
reciprocal appreciation and respect. Struggling together
means growing and bonding together. The goal is to
create shared memories that are the basis for stronger
relationships back at school. If Mohammed and his
classmates spend a week hiking, listening to the ghost
stories around the fire, and crossing the lake in a canoe,

they will develop bonds that will be not easily broken. And let's face it, if they can figure out how to traverse the ROPES course, then figuring out how to work together on a science project doesn't seem so challenging.

Paying Attention To Everyone's Unique Needs And Differences

For so long the onus for lack of friendships was placed squarely on the shoulders of students with disabilities. If only he could stop hitting, be more outgoing, act his age, then he could make friends. But as we spent time in schools talking to students, we stopped thinking in terms of "if only he could talk" and more in terms of "if only he wasn't pulled out of class so often."

However, we recognize the fact that individual differences and needs do play a part in how friendships come together. If you are, by nature or desire, a quiet person, you may be more likely to seek out others who share your love of silence. You may not be comfortable with the "on the run" conversations of a crowded, fast moving high school hallway or the hustle and bustle of the cafeteria. On the other hand, if you are active and have a tough time staying still for very long, you may find it hard to engage in quiet reflection with others who want to talk about their beliefs and ideals. Personal differences do make a difference.

As a strategy for supporting friendship, it is important to take these differences and needs into consideration. A student who uses facilitated communication (FC) to speak may not be able to carry on a conversation and eat lunch at the same time. Is this a problem? Of course not, unless we expect all friendships to include lively cafeteria discussion. A student with autism may want to swing alone during recess to clear her head and soothe her system. Again not a problem, unless we judge friendship by the social connections made during these times.

As one student told us, "When someone says 'hi' to me in the hallways, I want to respond, but by the time I get the words to come out of my mouth, he is already at the other end of the hall. This is who I am, and I need the kid who said 'hi' to know that I am not ignoring him."

Be Mindful of Groupings and Activities

Have you ever asked or been asked these questions?

◎ Is it better to invite one or more children over for a play date with my son?

◎ Should I arrange planned activities or let them fend for themselves?

◎ If another child invites my daughter over, should I suggest they get together at our home instead?

These are great questions, for they move us out of the realm of "can my son have friends?" and into the world of "what strategies make the most sense?" They also acknowledge that mindful intentionality is important.

But when we begin to answer these questions, we find ourselves hemming and hawing a bit. Not because we do not have experiences and opinions, but because we have learned that there are no hard and fast rules when it comes to these types of questions. Whether it is better to invite one or more children to play with your son really depends on your son. And you. How comfortable are you with a houseful of boys? Would your son find it easier to connect one-on-one, or is the pressure eased if several children come over? What do the other children think?

Should you arrange planned activities when your daughter has friends over the house? How old is your daughter? What do kids her age like to do? Is your daughter someone who prefers planned activities or would she rather be spontaneous? What would her friends prefer?

Do you see what we mean? There are no absolutes, but there *are* some gentle and flexible guidelines. We list some of them below with a reminder that what works for one situation does not necessarily work for another. Please consider these with caution and critical thought.

Structured To Free - Flowing

It often helps to first get kids together under the guise of a structured event or group, perhaps one that is school-sponsored, and then move into more free-flowing opportunities. For example, having students get together at a school dance, concert, or sporting event before just hanging out at the mall or the beach.

Adult Support Available but Not Intrusive

Adults can certainly get in the way of budding friendships but they can also be very helpful. Initially you may want to have an adult available, but only moving into the picture when truly necessary. Find an adult who is comfortable with this role, one who will be invisible when not needed.

Short Stints in the Beginning

When just getting to know someone, it is often helpful to have a time-limited first or second get-together. Better to leave wanting more than being anxious to get away.

Let the Student Shine

If you are going to help arrange some planned activities, choose at least one that allows the student to shine. This will help his new friends see him as skilled and passionate.

Truly Collaborative Activities

If you are going to arrange some planned activities, choose at least one that cannot be completed unless everyone contributes. For example, making pizzas so that everyone has a different ingredient to add. This will help ensure that all participate and are valued for contributions.

Identify Your Non-Negotiables

There may be some things that are your non-negotiables. Your son is on a sugar-free diet. Your student is allergic to peanuts. Your daughter cannot go swimming by herself. It is important to identify these and clearly communicate them to new friends. You need to feel confident that these non-negotiables will be respected at all times. But be careful about calling everything a non-negotiable. You may *want* your son to wear a hat when he goes outside but is this truly a non-negotiable? Too many non-negotiables and you may be scaring away potential friends.

No Litmus Test

Sure there are many things that you would like a new or potential friend to know and be comfortable doing. It would be great if friends knew how to support your son to use the bathroom or smoothly transfer between his wheelchair and the car. But unless these are your non-negotiables (and remember you should only have one or two of those) they do not need to immediately be put into the picture in a budding friendship. No one wants to feel they have to pass a test in order to get involved in a new relationship.

Develop Communication Supports

"Don't you need to be able to talk in order to have friends?" This was the question posed to us during a friendship workshop several years ago. The questioner was a very caring young teacher who was expressing what many in the audience were thinking: "Can you really be friends with someone who does not talk?"

We love this question for so many reasons. First, it reinforces how important it is to keep an open and honest dialogue when trying to figure out this beautiful but complex thing we call friendship. If the questioner did not feel she could ask this question then the opportunities for examining our core beliefs around love and friendship would be lost. Similarly, without a question like this, we might never fully explore the topic of communication, getting to the heart of how people communicate and our abilities to listen to more than just words. And lastly, this question challenges us. How do we support students to communicate in ways more easily understood by others, and what do we do when our supports are not enough?

First, let's look at our core beliefs about love and

friendship. Although this is a book about friendship, we haven't really written that much about what we think friendship is. That is deliberate. There are so many books written about the ins and outs and ups and down of love and relationships. As we often say, if we really understood what makes two people fall in love we would be on the *Oprah* show. And so we intentionally stay out of the "what makes a relationship" fray.

That said, we do have some strong beliefs about friendship and we do not think friendship is based on a specific skill or ability. We do not think people choose friends based on their abilities to sew or drive or speak Arabic or ride a horse. Granted, those qualities may be the impetus for meeting someone, but we do not believe love develops from those skills. Instead, we think relationships develop because of the intangibles: Caring. Good listener. Generosity. Sense of humor. Loving. Strength. Passion. Kindness. Challenging. Comfort.

Are we correct? It's impossible to say. But if we are, then the ability to speak is no more compulsory than the ability to bake a cake from scratch.

While the caring teacher framed the question specifically around being able to "talk," we think it is important to ask the question: "What is communication?" For it is said that even those of us who are fluent speakers use non-verbal communication far more than speech. Our behaviors, gestures, body language, and facial expressions are all ways in which we communicate what we are thinking, feeling, desiring. And we want people to listen to these in the same way as they listen to our words. And so when we meet a student who does not speak, or does not easily use speech, we cannot say she is not communicating. It is essential that we begin to learn how to listen to all of the ways each person communicates, and to teach students, colleagues and families to do the same. If we really "learn to listen," as the late Herb Lovett advocated, we might find ourselves more likely to see the possibilities of friendship with someone who does not speak.

But of course, we must always ask ourselves how we support each and every student to have more effective ways to communicate. In this day and age, with daily technological breakthroughs, any student not able to fully communicate can and should be supported to develop alternative and augmentative forms of communication

(AAC). All students should get this respect and commitment to develop ways to communicate everything that in their minds and hearts.

And if we don't succeed? If we are not able to come up with a form of AAC that allows that student to express her thoughts and desires in complex and consistent ways? We keep trying, we never give up. But we also do not fall into the trap of thinking that because that student does not yet have a way for us to understand exactly what is in her mind, that she is any less a person or would be any less a wonderful friend. What we believe about students for whom communication remains a challenge is perhaps the greatest indication or our beliefs around belonging and community.

 ## Be Like Water Revisited

We end the *Strategies* section by revisiting some earlier advice: As you move forward on the path of supporting friendships for the students you know and love, you will surely bump into many obstacles along the way. You may be told you are wrong or naïve or that you have your head in the clouds. You might find that some of the strategies backfire or stall or just don't work out the way you hoped or planned. You will certainly run into barriers that push against strategies and make it seem as if what you are trying to accomplish is just plain impossible. You may go home and shake your head and wonder if it is really worth it after all.

As so once again we remind you: *Be Like Water*. For no matter the obstacle, water never stops pushing onward. It goes under, over, even through whatever stands in its way. It doesn't give up, it keeps going until it gets to where it has to be. And as long as we keep our eyes on the prize of friendship, we will never stop moving forward until we get to where we have to be.

CONCLUSION

by Jamie Burke

My experience in the form of a young man living with autism means to me a different appearance of looking at life. Of course, my method of communicating through typing brings many challenges, although mostly not to me, but to others who must accept and believe in it. I truly think my peers are not as challenged as many adults I have worked with. So, looking differently suggests to those with typical lifestyles that meeting and maintaining a friendship is a simple truth.

The road to the dream of lives filled with friends, dates, and girls implies the best of life. That road, however, at times can be treacherous with heartache and hope. I am certain that we desire what gives emotions the places to experience them. Adults help by giving us signs that may be as guides to figuring out where we need to go and what to do to head in the right direction. Many times it seems I get uncertain.

Friendships seem to require only a mutual desire and a heart open enough to a great new opportunity. It seems a simple statement. We are willing and ready to connect with other kids, and adults must quietly step into the background, camouflaging their help as a tiger who may hide in full view. It's the needed disguise of the adult who smoothes the way with the friendship, then stands back in the shadows, observing the complicated dance of steps taking you to the feeling of confidence. Once you have experienced the joy of being included and valued, it's hard to accept when it does not connect again in similar fashion if that friendship takes a leave of absence. When the process begins it again, it can try the soul to tread over this familiar territory yet again. The person who is supporting the process must know that it is a strong human desire of everyone to share lives and secret dreams and humorous laughter. I want nothing less for myself than what my brothers experience, and I think people may assume that if we cannot outwardly speak this to others, that we are content to sit back and stay in the shadows. Let me say explicitly, we are not.

I am certain as lives move into the era of journeying hand-in-hand, with eyes looking to think with lucid, clear goals to what will change society into one that opens doors and not to just slip through with no struggles, but to make it wide open, letting all ease joyously through. Waiting on the other side of that door will be groups of all kinds, sharing, laughing and loving all that life enjoins. That is my dream for all.

References and Other Helpful Resources

Amado, A. N. (1993). *Friendships and community connections between people with and without developmental disabilities.* Baltimore: Paul H. Brookes Publishing Co.

Armstrong, T. (1994). *Multiple intelligences in the classroom.* Alexandria, VA: Association for Supervision and Curriculum Development.

Biklen, D. (Ed). (2005). *Autism and the myth of the person alone.* New York: New York University Press.

Bogdan, R. & Biklen, D. (1977). Handicapism. *Social Policy,* March/April, 14-19.

Bogdan, R. & Taylor, S. J. (1989). Relationships with severely disabled people: The social construction of humanness. *Social Problems, 36:2,* 135-148.

Brendtro, L., Brokenleg, M., Van Bockern, S. (1990). *Reclaiming youth at risk: Our hope for the future.* Bloomington, IN: National Educational Service.

Brown, C. (1955). *My Left Foot.* New York: Simon & Schuster.

Causton-Theoharis, J., & Malmgren, K. (2005). Increasing peer interactions for students with severe disabilities via paraprofessional training. *Exceptional Children, 71,* 431-444.

Crossley, R. (1997). *Speechless: Facilitating communication for people without voices.* New York: Dutton.

Desmond-Hurst, B. (Producer & Director). (1951). *Scrooge (A Christmas Carol-* United States) [Motion Picture]. United Kingdom: Renown Pictures Corporation LTD.

Disney, W. (Producer), & Geronimi, C., Jackson, W., & Luske, H. (Directors). (1953). *Peter Pan* [Motion Picture]. United States: Walt Disney Productions.

Donnellan, A. M., & Leary, M. R. (1995). *Movement differences in autism/mental retardation: Appreciating and accommodating people with communication and behavior challenges.* Madison, WI: DRI Press.

Evans, I. M., & Meyer, L. H. (2001). Having friends and Rett syndrome: How social relationships create meaningful contexts for limited skills. *Disability and Rehabilitation, 23,* 167-176.

Falvey, M. A., Forest, M., Pearpoint, J., & Rosenberg, R. (1994). *All my life's a circle. Using the tools: Circles, MAP's and PATH.* Toronto: Inclusion Press.

Fisher, R., & Ury, W. (1983). *Getting to yes: Negotiating agreement without giving in.* New York: Penguin Books.

Giangreco, M. F., Luiselli, T. E., & MacFarland, S. Z. C. (1997). Helping or hovering? Effects of instructional assistant proximity on students with disabilities. *Exceptional Children, 64,* 7-18.

Giangreco, M. F., Broer, S. M., & Edelman, S. W. (2001). Teacher engagement with students with disabilities: Differences between paraprofessional service delivery models. *Journal of the Association for Persons with Severe Handicaps, 26,* 75-86.

Guber, Peter (Producer), & Levinson, B. (Director). (1988). *Rain Man* [Motion Picture]. United States: Mirage Entertainment.

Hadary, H., & Whiteford, W. (Producers) & Whiteford, W. (Director). (1999). *King Gimp* [Motion Picture]. United States: Whiteford-Hadary Productions.

Heller, P. & Morrison, S. (Producers), & Sheridan, J. (Director). (1989). *My Left Foot* [Motion Picture]. United States: Ferndale Films.

Holt, K. W. (1998). *My Louisiana Sky.* New York: Dell Yearling.

Jackson, L. (2002). *Freaks, geeks, & Asperger syndrome.* London: Jessica Kingsley Publishers.

Jones, R. (1976). *The acorn people*. New York: Bantam Doubleday Dell Books for Young Readers.

Kishi, G., & Meyer, L. (1994). What children report and remember: A six-year follow-up of the effects of social contact between peers with and without severe disabilities. *JASH, 19*, 277-289.

Kunc, N. (1992). The need to belong: Rediscovering Maslow's hierarchy of needs. In R. Villa, J. Thousand, W. Stainback & S. Stainback (Eds.) *Restructuring for caring & effective education: An administrative guide to creating heterogeneous schools*. Baltimore: Paul H. Brookes Publishing Co.

Lovett, H. (1996). *Learning to listen: Positive approaches and people with difficult behavior*. Baltimore: Paul H. Brookes.

Lutfiyya, Z. M. (1991). "A feeling of being connected": Friendships between people with and without learning difficulties. *Disability, Handicap & Society, 6*, 233-245.

Martin, J., Tashie, C., & Nisbet, J. (Producers), & Samson, G. (Director). (1996). *Voices of Friendship* [Video Documentary]. United States: Institute on Disability/UCE, University of New Hampshire.

Maslow, A.H. (1943). A theory of human motivation. *Psychological Review, 50*, 370-396.

Murray-Seegert, C. (1989). *Nasty girls, thugs, and humans like us: Social relations between severely disabled and nondisabled students in high school*. Baltimore: Paul H. Brookes Publishing Co.

Newton, C., & Wilson, D. (2003). *Creating circles of friends: A peer support and inclusion workbook*. Inclusive Solutions UK Limited.

Pakula, A. J. (Producer), & Mulligan, R. (Director). (1962). *To Kill a Mockingbird* [Motion Picture]. United States: Universal International Pictures.

Perske, R. (1988). *Circles of friends: People with disabilities and their friends enrich the lives of one another.* Nashville: Abingdon Press.

Schaffner, C. B., & Buswell, B. (1992). *Connecting students: A guide to thoughtful friendship facilitation for educators & families.* Colorado Springs, CO: PEAK Parent Center.

Schnorr, R. (1990). "Peter? He comes and goes...": First graders' perspectives on a part-time mainstream student. *Journal of the Association for Persons with Severe Handicaps, 15,* 231-240.

Schnorr, R. (1997). From enrollment to membership: "Belonging" in middle and high school classes. *Journal of the Association for Persons with Severe Handicaps, 22,* 1-15.

Shapiro, J. P. (1993). *No pity: People with disabilities forging a new civil rights movement.* New York: Times Books.

Sienkiewicz-Mercer, R., & Kaplan, S. B. (1989). *I raise my eyes to say yes: A memoir.* West Hartford, CT: Whole Health Books.

Snell, M. & Janney, R. (2000). *Teachers' guides to inclusive practices: Social relationships and peer support.* Baltimore: Paul H. Brookes Publishing Co.

Staub, D. (1998). *Delicate threads: Friendships between children with and without special needs in inclusive settings.* Bethesda, MD: Woodbine House.

Strully, J., & Strully, C. (1992). That which binds us: Friendship as a safe harbor in a storm. In A. N. Amado (Ed.) *Friendships and community connections between people with and without developmental disabilities* (pp.213-225). Baltimore: Paul H. Brookes Publishing Co.

Tomlinson, C. A. (1999). *The differentiated classroom: Responding to the needs of all learners.* Alexandria, VA: Association for Supervision and Curriculum Development.

Trueman, T. (2000). *Stuck in neutral.* New York: Harper Collins Publishers.

Van der Klift, E. & Kunc, N. (2002). Beyond benevolence: Supporting genuine friendships in inclusive schools. In J.S. Thousand, R.A. Villa, & A.I. Nevin (Eds.) *Creativity and collaborative learning: A practical guide to empowering students and teachers.* Baltimore: Paul H. Brookes Publishing Co.

Films Related to Disability and Friendship

Major Motion Pictures

50 First Dates (2004)
Benny and Joon (1993)
Dance Me to My Song (1998)
Elling (2001)
Finding Nemo (2003)
Profoundly Normal (2003)
Pumpkin (2002)
Rory O'Shea Was Here (2004)
The Station Agent (2003)

Documentaries

Autism is a World (2004)
King Gimp (1999)
Liebe Perla (1999)
My Flesh and Blood (2003)
Twitch and Shout (1993)
Voices of Friendship (1996)
When Billy Broke his Head...and other Tales of Wonder (1995)